Im
Le

in
Schools

ISBN 0 1149 7292 3

Contents

Foreword

High quality leadership is a key component of effective schools. The impact of leadership on pupils' learning and attainment is regularly demonstrated in HMI inspection reports on schools across Scotland. *Standards and Quality in Scottish Schools 1995-1998* reported that the leadership of headteachers was very good or showed more strengths than weaknesses in 80 per cent of primary schools and 85 per cent of secondary schools. Similar patterns were shown for leadership at other levels of the school's organisation.

Where effective leadership is in place, the impact on pupils' learning is significant and demonstrable. However, where leadership is not sufficiently developed or well focused, pupils' learning experiences invariably suffer and in many schools there is clearly scope for improving the quality of leadership.

Successful school management has many features but we need to give more attention to the role of leadership throughout the organisation. The leadership skills of headteachers are particularly important but many other teachers have leadership roles in departments, curriculum areas, pupil support and in taking forward whole-school developments. Effective leadership in all these aspects of the school's work can make a real difference to the quality of pupils' experience.

High quality school leaders are not designated at birth but develop their skills progressively throughout their careers. Many readers will recall the benefits from working with colleagues who provided clear leadership. Similarly, teachers, in developing their career, need suitable opportunities to take a lead role and develop some of the key skills required. The Scottish Qualification for Headship is a recognition of the importance of such effective preparation for leading a school.

This publication identifies ten characteristics of the most effective leadership in schools. These characteristics include the importance of having a vision for the school and a strong focus on the core business of learning and teaching. Overall, the characteristics emphasise the fact that school management has to be much more than efficient day-to-day administration. The characteristics are derived from effective leadership which inspectors have seen in many different types of schools and contexts across Scotland. A small sample of these real examples is included as case studies which demonstrate the leadership characteristics in action.

It is important that education authorities and schools continue to raise awareness of the importance of school leadership, evaluate the quality of leadership in place and identify practical ways of securing improvements. This publication is designed to assist in this process. Further improving leadership in Scottish schools is one major way in which we can secure significant benefits for pupils' learning and attainment.

Douglas A Osler
HM Senior Chief Inspector of Schools

Acknowledgements

These materials were developed by the HMI Quality, Standards and Audit Division in partnership with the staff in each of the case study schools and their respective education authorities.

In addition, valuable comments on the materials were provided by members of a reference group set up to assist in developing the publication:

David Cameron, Area Education Manager, Fife Council

Mike McCabe, Director of Education, South Ayrshire Council

Len McConnell, Head of Service, Educational Development, Perth and Kinross

Dr Jenny Reeves, National Development Officer, Scottish Qualification for Headship.

1 ⋯⋗ **Improving Leadership**

1. Improving Leadership

1.1 Introduction

Improving Leadership in Scottish Schools is designed for use by education authority officers, school managers and teachers who are concerned to review and develop aspects of leadership, management and quality assurance.

This publication is intended to be used within the overall approach to school self-evaluation set out in *How good is our school*?. The emphasis throughout is on the specific performance indicator **7.4 Effectiveness of Leadership**, within the wider context of the key area of management, leadership and quality assurance. The main focus is on the leadership of headteachers. However, the key characteristics of very good leadership and the approaches to self-evaluation exemplified are also applicable to a wide range of other posts where effective leadership is required. These materials, therefore, should make a useful contribution to the staff development and review process in schools and education authorities in a wide range of settings.

Self-evaluation is part of the wider process of development planning. It is designed to:

- improve the quality of experience of the young people in our schools
- raise attainment.

How good is our school? indicates that an overview of issues should take place on a regular basis. This overview should draw information, as appropriate, from the following:

- the headteacher
- senior promoted staff
- individual departments or stages
- learning support and guidance staff
- groups of staff
- staff giving an individual response
- pupils
- parents.

This publication aims to address key issues surrounding leadership and management and provides materials which are designed to help you to:

- reflect upon key aspects of leadership
- distinguish aspects of leadership from related management skills
- identify some of the main attributes of good leadership
- evaluate the quality of leadership in schools
- identify steps which can be taken to improve the quality and effectiveness of leadership in schools.

1.2. Leadership in Schools

Effective headteachers provide high quality leadership. They are the driving force in taking a school forward and in harnessing the energies of staff, pupils and the wider community. They play a key role in identifying and implementing initiatives in order to continuously improve the quality of learning, teaching and attainment in their schools. Many other members of staff also have important leadership roles and need to display leadership qualities. For example, members of senior management teams, principal teachers in secondary schools, senior teachers in primary schools and team leaders in special schools all have key leadership responsibilities. Within any school, individual staff will therefore be at different stages in the development of leadership qualities.

Effective leadership and effective management are often found together. The Standard for Headship in Scotland (SHS) defines the key purpose of headship as:

> "To provide the leadership and management which enables a school to give every pupil high quality education and which promotes the highest possible standards of achievement".

Of course, a headteacher's vision and leadership skills need to be complemented by well-developed management expertise if a school is to be successful. Vision without a detailed grasp of the means of implementation may quickly result in a headteacher being characterised as having their 'head in the clouds' or being 'out of touch with reality'. Similarly, day-to-day management expertise alone, without effective leadership, may result in a school which runs quite efficiently but lacks an overall sense of purpose and strategic direction.

The Standard identifies the balance required from an effective headteacher:

> "working in partnership with staff, parents, pupils and the wider community, the headteacher must articulate a vision and give direction to the school which will lead to effective learning and teaching ………
> In consultation with all those with an interest in the school, she/he must be able to create, develop and review the aims, plans, policies and procedures which will translate that vision into everyday reality".

This balance of qualities also reflects the leadership criteria identified within the excellence model of the European Foundation for Quality Management (EFQM).

1.3 Leadership and Management

Leadership and management are closely related concepts. In much of the literature, leadership is regarded as a key part of management. However, inspection evidence has suggested that, in some schools, managers tend to over-emphasise the day-to-day administrative functions of their roles rather than giving sufficient attention to the key aspects of providing more strategic leadership. In such schools, management may be associated mainly with planning, organising, deploying and monitoring the use of staff and other resources. Leadership is an essential requirement of providing a more strategic approach to management. Leadership has many aspects but involves developing, sharing and sustaining a vision based on shared values, providing clear direction and motivating others.

Whilst leadership and management skills are complementary and closely linked, it is important to distinguish between them clearly. In everyday language, it is common to talk about 'providing a lead'. However, we often recognise that someone can be an effective operational manager or administrator whilst not necessarily being an effective leader. Here it may be more common to refer to someone 'managing on a day-to-day basis', 'managing the budget' or 'managing resources'. We tend not to use 'leading' in these instances.

Leadership, therefore, is closely related to strategic management but distinguishable from more operational and administrative management tasks in a number of key respects:

- **Leadership is about setting out and inspiring others with a longer-term strategic vision for the future**; without such leadership, management tends to have a narrow and restrictive focus on the day-to-day.

- **Leadership is about challenging and changing some of the key priorities**; without such leadership, management tends to focus more on the best use of available resources to meet a specific priority.

- **Leadership is about setting and reviewing objectives in relation to a clear strategic view of what is to be achieved**; without such leadership, management may focus mainly on setting up systems to take forward particular objectives without questioning their appropriateness.

- **Leadership involves winning hearts and minds and inspiring others to want to perform consistently to the highest standards**; without such leadership, management may be more concerned with setting out and monitoring operational guidelines which restrict innovation and creativity rather than empowering staff to perform.

- **Leadership involves looking beyond the school and working with others who can contribute to school improvement**; without such leadership, management may tend to evaluate success against a limited and inward-looking view of what is possible.

- **Leadership sets out and builds an over-arching school ethos of achievement and success**; without such leadership, management may focus only on means of monitoring and tracking performance, without promoting improvement.

The next section develops main aspects of leadership further and suggests ten key characteristics which can be used as a framework for improving its effectiveness.

2 ∙∙∙⟩ **Some Key Issues in Leadership**

2. Some Key Issues in Leadership

2.1 Evidence from School Inspections

Evidence from school inspections across Scotland has demonstrated the crucial importance of effective leadership to the success of pupils and schools. *Standards and Quality in Scottish Schools 1995-1998* reported that the leadership of headteachers was very good or showed more strengths than weaknesses in 80 per cent of primary schools and 85 per cent of secondary schools. Promoted staff, other than headteachers, were effective in 85 per cent of primary schools. In 75 per cent of secondary schools, the senior management team's contribution to the effectiveness of the school was very good or had more strengths than weaknesses. The leadership of principal teachers in secondary schools was very good in 30 per cent of departments and had more strengths than weaknesses in a further 45 per cent. However, inspection evidence was equally clear that in a significant minority of primary and secondary schools aspects of leadership required to be improved. In these schools, weaknesses in leadership at headteacher and other levels could have very adverse effects on the quality of pupils' learning and attainment.

In the most effective schools and departments, leaders established a positive ethos of achievement and provided staff and pupils with frequent feedback on their work. Up-to-date knowledge of the curriculum and key educational developments were used to articulate a clear vision and a well-judged pace of development. Effective leaders took care to consult widely with staff in order to build a shared understanding of the school or department's work, and to recognise the value of everybody's contribution to it. However, they also did not shy away from taking and explaining difficult, and sometimes unpopular, decisions when necessary.

Very good leaders demonstrated each day their awareness of the importance of setting a personal example of commitment and enthusiasm to promote similar attributes amongst staff and pupils. They were readily accessible to pupils, parents and staff, but remained proactive in their work, rather than simply reacting to the particular problems of the day.

The best leaders demonstrated high levels of awareness of the need to develop leadership skills in other staff. They encouraged and empowered their colleagues to take forward their remits imaginatively. Decision-making was delegated clearly and appropriately, with leaders keen to build teamwork and a sense of common purpose. Responsibilities for assisting staff in their professional development were taken very seriously.

Where necessary, effective leaders in schools demonstrated that they were prepared to challenge any staff who did not meet the standards set by consistently setting out the improvements required and taking appropriate steps to help them do so.

Inspection evidence from schools with high quality leadership demonstrated that the influence of effective leadership and vision could be clearly traced in all aspects of school life. In the best examples, leadership was particularly well focused on the central concern of developing learning and teaching and pupils' attainment. In this respect, it is important to note that the performance indicators set out in *How good is our school?* are necessarily inter-related in a number of important ways. Performance indicator 7.4 on the Effectiveness of Leadership cannot be judged in isolation from the levels awarded in other performance indicators across the seven Key Areas. Particularly relevant to the overall evaluation of the quality of school leadership are the performance indicators covering:

- Structure of the curriculum (PI 1.1)
- Overall quality of attainment (PI 2.3)
- Quality of the teaching process (PI 3.1)
- Quality of pupils' learning (PI 3.2)
- Meeting pupils' needs (PI 3.3)
- Ethos (PI 5.1)
- Self-evaluation (PI 7.1)
- The development plan (PI 7.2)
- Implementing the development plan (P1 7.3).

The overall quality of leadership within a school or department should be closely related to the quality of performance across this set of indicators. Effective leaders who have been in post for a reasonable time need to have demonstrated that they have made a difference in most or all of these core aspects of a school's or department's work (see Appendix 3, page 62).

The related set of case studies (pages 67-113) are selected to illustrate the impact effective leadership can have across a number of these specific aspects of a school's work.

2.2 Ten Characteristics of Effective Leadership and Sources of Evidence

What then are the main characteristics of effective leadership, whether demonstrated by headteachers or other staff with leadership roles in schools? Evidence from school inspections and other research suggests that the best leaders are likely to demonstrate strong performance across **10 key characteristics**.

1. Building alliances within and beyond the school

2. Being committed and purposeful

3. Developing teamwork

4. Developing and sharing a vision

5. Focusing on learning

6. Demonstrating interpersonal skills

7. Developing personal credibility

8. Prioritising

9. Being responsive

10. Delegating and sharing leadership.

These characteristics are not listed in any hierarchical order and have some inevitable overlaps. Overall, however, these features encompass many of the strengths of the best leaders seen in a wide range of inspections in primary, secondary and special schools.

Effective leadership is so important to schools that we need clear evidence that it is happening. We therefore need to consider in greater detail how a school can establish the extent to which these characteristics are being displayed by its leaders. The following tables take the ten key characteristics in turn and consider what each of them might look like in practice. They also consider the sources of evidence you might use to help make an evaluation of each of them.

Ten Characteristics of Effective School Leadership

Characteristics Of Effective Leaders	Sources Of Evidence
1. Building alliances within and beyond the school Effective leaders: • understand the context of their schools and systematically seek out and develop productive partnerships in the immediate and wider community • recognise their need for support, challenge and stimulation through actively seeking feedback from others who are external to the school • recognise the contribution of others to the school's activities and the part the school can play in meeting the needs and expectations of the community.	What are the sources of advice and development for the headteacher and other leaders in the school? What form do they take? How often are meetings held with sources of external advice and support? What changes have they brought about? How open are leaders to constructive criticism? What networks is the school a part of? Do leaders explicitly recognise priorities in the wider community? How many people or agencies do they meet with on a regular basis? What is the purpose and product of these relationships? Do leaders see links with other agencies as an end in themselves or do they use them to drive forward the school's main priorities?
2. Being committed and purposeful Effective leaders: • demonstrate a clear sense of purpose, and the energy and drive to get things done • are careful to share the purpose with others and to build wide support • are proactive in identifying areas for improvement • demonstrate strong personal commitment to key priorities such as improving learning and teaching and pupils' attainment • show drive and commitment that inspires and motivates others to give of their best • have a strong commitment to high standards in all aspects of the work of the school and act upon the findings of self-evaluation.	How do others view the commitment and purpose of school leaders? Does their energy and drive have a positive effect on others? How purposefully are the main priorities being taken forward? What examples have there been of the headteacher and other leaders in the school being proactive in school improvement? How clear and high are their expectations? Are there examples of committed leadership achieving successful outcomes for pupils and for the wider school community?

Characteristics Of Effective Leaders	Sources Of Evidence
3. Developing teamwork Effective leaders: ● build effective teams ● select, develop and promote staff through well-founded knowledge of their complementary, as well as their individual, strengths ● use conflicts of views constructively to promote professional growth and to negotiate a new consensus on the way forward.	How many identifiable teams are there in the school? Do leaders value different individual strengths and contributions in the membership of teams? Do they encourage teachers to collaborate in their work and observe one another teaching? Do leaders sustain teamwork through conflicts of view? Do they strike a balance among command, consultation and consensus, and between working directly with people and paper? Do they accurately identify the development needs of staff and ensure they are effectively met in staff development programmes?
4. Developing and sharing a vision Effective leaders: ● look beyond the present circumstances and help others to embrace a strategic educational vision of the future which takes appropriate account of the views and needs of a range of stakeholders in the school community ● plan collaboratively to make the vision a reality by setting short and medium-term targets, but are prepared for, and welcome, the unexpected ● give a high priority to communicating the vision to a wide audience.	Have leaders effectively developed and communicated a vision for the next three/five/ten years? Who has been involved in shaping it? How clearly do staff recognise and speak about the vision? Have leaders set the school's short and medium-term targets? What unexpected events have occurred recently? What are the unforeseen trends? How have they been dealt with by school leaders?
5. Focusing on learning Effective leaders: ● recognise pupils' learning as their 'core business' and put it at the centre of their management activities ● consistently encourage talk about learning and teaching and promote a climate of evaluation, inquiry and creativity to seek further improvements in overall quality.	How much of the leader's time is spent directly on core issues to do with pupils' learning? What strategies are used to promote a climate of learning across the school? To what extent do people talk about learning in the school on a day-to-day basis? What evidence is there of teachers as learners and of the school as a learning organisation? What evidence is there that high priority is given to monitoring classroom practice?

Characteristics Of Effective Leaders	Sources Of Evidence
6. Demonstrating interpersonal skills Effective leaders: ● understand their own strengths and weaknesses and are consistent ● understand issues from the point of view of other people and value their views and feelings ● are accessible, communicate well and are good listeners ● are confident in their role, reliable, and clear about their own educational values ● give high priority to building confidence and self-esteem in others and to helping colleagues to develop and contribute to school improvement ● accentuate the positive, provide praise and encouragement, and defuse potential problems and conflicts.	How do others perceive the strengths and weaknesses of school leadership? How do leaders in the school see themselves? How accessible are leaders seen to be? What are the most recent examples of communication and listening? How effective were they? What examples are there of developing the skills of others? What examples are there of promoting a positive atmosphere, providing praise and resolving difficulties?
7. Developing personal credibility Effective leaders: ● regularly demonstrate effective professional expertise in their day-to-day work ● are a source of reliable information and advice on educational practice ● demonstrate 'hands-on' leadership and a practical ability to translate aims into reality ● are a model of good practice for the staff and community and have gained their trust ● are principled and clearly demonstrate professional integrity ● reflect on and improve the effectiveness of their own leadership.	How are leaders demonstrating their effectiveness around the school? Are they effective teachers? Are they widely respected by pupils, staff and the wider community? Are they involved with others in 'hands on' development to move key priorities forward? Is their involvement valued by others? Are they seen as sources of practical advice and information? Have they earned the trust of others? Have they been effective in evaluating and improving their own leadership?

Characteristics Of Effective Leaders	Sources Of Evidence
8. Prioritising Effective leaders: • are very clear about what matters most and where their time will be used to best effect • reflect their strategic priorities through their day-to-day practice, time management and their commitment to continuous improvement.	How do leaders in the school, at whatever level, describe their key priorities? What do others (insiders and visitors) see as the main objectives in the school? What do teachers and pupils see as the main concerns of the headteacher and senior management? What examples are there of leaders giving a high priority to continuous improvement? What evidence is there of effective time management to support strategic priorities?
9. Being responsive Effective leaders: • listen carefully to pupils, staff, parents and the wider community and keep closely in touch with emerging issues and needs • respond flexibly and creatively but with an uncompromising stance on standards and quality.	Do staff, pupils, parents and the wider community feel that school leaders provide sufficient opportunities for their voices to be heard? What is the evidence of leaders taking action following consultation? What recent examples can be found which illustrate flexibility and responsiveness? What are seen as barriers to improvement? How positively do school leaders identify ways to overcome the barriers? Do they consistently maintain a focus on standards and quality?
10. Delegating and sharing leadership Effective leaders: • delegate effectively and positively by recognising the strengths and development needs of others • create freedom for focusing leadership on learning and teaching by delegating and streamlining subsidiary administrative tasks • use every opportunity to allow others to exercise leadership and to be innovative • know when to lead and when to draw on the leadership of others with evident strengths in particular areas.	What are seen as key management decisions? Who takes them? Who exercises leadership roles in the school? To what extent are there leadership opportunities for unpromoted staff and for pupils? How do people perceive and talk about leadership in the school?

2.3 What Effective School Leaders Do

These ten key characteristics of effective leadership are closely inter-related and sometimes overlap. However, evidence from inspections and research shows that high quality leadership in schools becomes evident in many ways.

Effective schools require leadership to be demonstrated at a number of levels, not just by the headteacher. Within their particular roles, school leaders are most effective when they:

- develop a clear and rational vision which commands wide support
- become proactive in implementing change
- ensure teamwork is ever more important
- use persuasion and influence rather than authority
- understand and treat staff as valued individuals, not resources
- create a strong sense of team spirit based on mutual trust, respect and support
- consistently raise the expectations staff and pupils have of themselves
- inspire and empower staff and pupils to make a difference
- consistently challenge and support staff.

Effective school leaders recognise that an important part of their role is to share their aims and vision in a way which will inspire staff and pupils to be part of it. They take frequent opportunities to:

- express and promote their educational vision and goals in an exciting way
- make sure that all staff and pupils can meet their individual objectives as part of the well-defined collective purpose of the school
- recognise and emphasise the accomplishments of others as part of building an ethos of achievement
- avoid a 'culture of blame' by treating problems and setbacks as opportunities for individuals and the organisation to learn and improve.

Effective school leaders have a good awareness of their own strengths and development needs. They are quick to recognise the strengths of others and take appropriate steps to make sure that potential is realised. On a school or departmental basis they:

- stimulate staff and pupils' imaginations about what can be achieved
- identify and develop everybody's potential

- delegate challenging and rewarding tasks
- delegate some of the power and authority to decide
- provide the stimulus and encouragement for staff and pupils to take maximum responsibility for managing themselves.

School leaders who have well-developed approaches to their roles which reflect many of these themes generally have very high professional credibility and are well placed to take forward school improvement. How then can leadership be evaluated and further developed in schools? The next section outlines the processes for your own school and follows a fictional example, Anytown School.

development

prioritising

credibility

communication

3 ⋯⋗ **Evaluating and Improving Leadership in Schools –**
An Introduction to Materials for Staff Development and Self-Evaluation

motivation

teamwork

interpersonal skills

focus

delegating

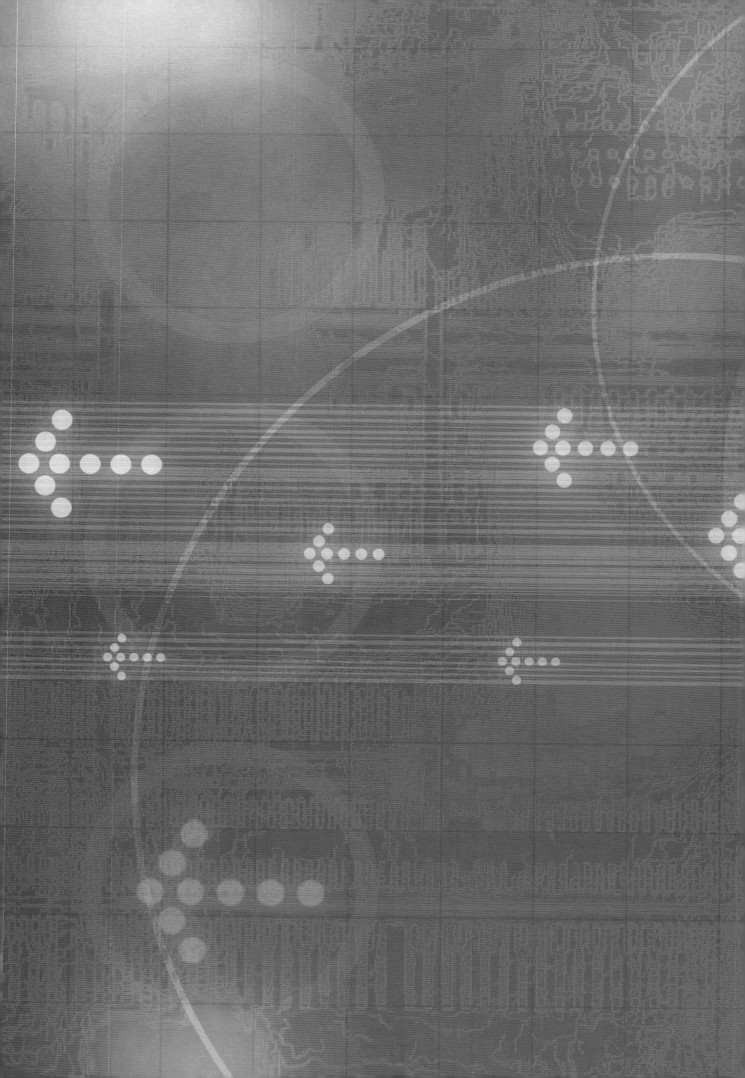

3. Evaluating and Improving Leadership in Schools

3.1 Using the Staff Development Materials to Evaluate and Improve Leadership in Your Own School

Improving Leadership in Scottish Schools is designed to be used alongside *How good is our school?* and other relevant publications. A set of staff development activities is provided on pages 35-46 and on pages 69-70 to help you evaluate and improve leadership in your own school. These staff development materials suggest practical activities for use during in-service sessions organised, for example, by:

- education authorities as part of targeted leadership courses
- schools
- individuals
- management teams
- departments
- other school teams.

They can be used as they stand or edited and adapted to suit the needs of your own school. They can be used and adapted to raise awareness of the importance of leadership at a range of levels within schools.

They use the structure of the three questions from *How good is our school?*:

- **How are we doing?**
- **How do we know?**
- **What are we going to do now?**

To answer the first two questions, the materials show you how to take a **broad view** across a number of areas and then a **closer look** at some of these, using the performance indicators to help you.

To answer the third question, the materials illustrate an approach that you might use to move forward from evaluating the evidence to create action plans for improvement. You are also encouraged to make **selective** use of the leadership case studies on pages 67-113 which exemplify how others, in leadership roles in contrasting contexts, have developed their own leadership and made a real difference to their schools.

To assist you in using these staff development activities in your own school, worked examples have been included based on Anytown School (pages 25-32). These examples illustrate a sequence of staff development on leadership in a fictional school which continues from the **broad view** until an action plan is produced.

3.2 Summary of the Evaluation and Improvement Process

The process of carrying out an evaluation on leadership is described for both Anytown School and your own school. It follows the approach set out in Part 2 of *How good is our school?*.

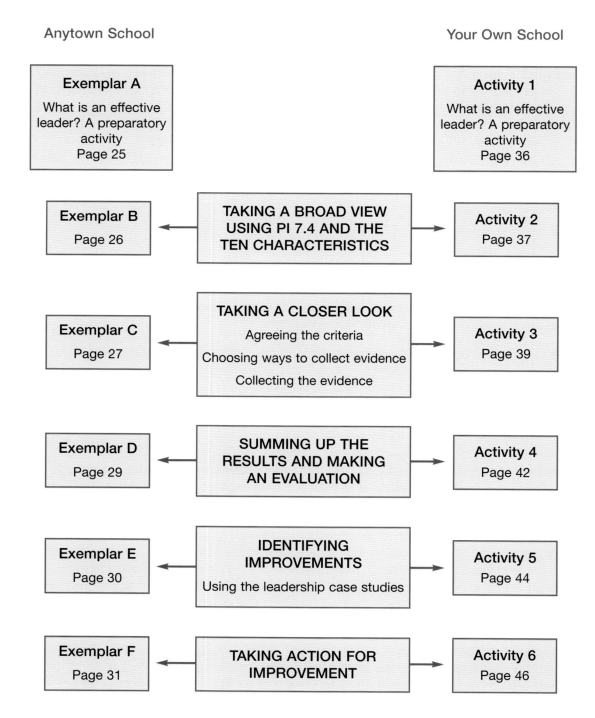

Anytown School   Your Own School

Exemplar A

What is an effective leader? A preparatory activity
Page 25

Activity 1

What is an effective leader? A preparatory activity
Page 36

Exemplar B

Page 26

TAKING A BROAD VIEW USING PI 7.4 AND THE TEN CHARACTERISTICS

Activity 2

Page 37

Exemplar C

Page 27

TAKING A CLOSER LOOK

Agreeing the criteria

Choosing ways to collect evidence

Collecting the evidence

Activity 3

Page 39

Exemplar D

Page 29

SUMMING UP THE RESULTS AND MAKING AN EVALUATION

Activity 4

Page 42

Exemplar E

Page 30

IDENTIFYING IMPROVEMENTS

Using the leadership case studies

Activity 5

Page 44

Exemplar F

Page 31

TAKING ACTION FOR IMPROVEMENT

Activity 6

Page 46

development

prioritising

credibility

communication

4 **Evaluating and Improving Leadership in Schools**
Anytown School Exemplar Materials

motivation

teamwork

interpersonal skills

focus

delegating

4. Evaluating and Improving Leadership in Schools - Anytown School Exemplar Materials

4.1 Exemplar A: Awareness Raising; What Is an Effective Leader?

The headteacher of Anytown School used the set of slides (Appendix 1, pages 49–60) to introduce staff to aspects of leadership and the ten key characteristics.

To further raise awareness of the importance of leadership across the staff and consider the criteria to use to judge the effectiveness of leadership at the various levels within the school, the staff of Anytown School undertook various group activities:

A   They identified the main characteristics staff valued in an effective school leader. Staff groups agreed on five characteristics which they considered to be the key to effective leadership. The criteria from each group were collected and collated.

B   Staff focused on the ten key characteristics of effective leadership set out in this document. Through discussion, staff put these ten characteristics into priority order and considered whether any other aspects required to be added. The findings of the school groups were discussed and a collated version agreed.

From the awareness-raising activities, staff gained a clearer idea of the importance of leadership at all levels in the school. At the headteacher's request, they then moved to consider aspects of his/her leadership.

4.2 Exemplar B: Taking A Broad View of Leadership Using PI 7.4 and the Ten Leadership Characteristics [Anytown School]

Anytown School is setting out to look at leadership at all levels in the school. The headteacher felt that the best way to begin the process was to start with his/her own leadership.

The PI grid below shows the collated evidence which has been gathered from a **scan across the three themes of PI 7.4**. The level of performance assigned to each of the themes has been agreed and is shown. It is important to note that account was taken of other PI evidence such as those suggested on page 10.

The levels of performance are those set out in *How good is our school?*: 4 = very good (major strengths); 3 = good (strengths outweigh weaknesses); 2 = fair (some important weaknesses); 1 = unsatisfactory (major weaknesses).

Anytown School: Leadership of the headteacher

	Management, Leadership & Quality Assurance	Performance Indicator Theme	Level	Evidence to make this judgement
7.4	Effectiveness of leadership	• professional competence and commitment	4	Most staff believe that the headteacher is committed to the school and provides an effective professional example. He/she is good at prioritising, initiating and directing projects for improvement. He/she manages staff effectively and supports staff development. He/she has demonstrated and assisted others by very good up-to-date knowledge of current developments in education.
		• leadership qualities	2	Some staff feel the headteacher creates confidence. Most see him/her as approachable and responsive. Many agree he/she is a good listener but not always a good communicator. Few are aware of the school's vision. The headteacher is only involved periodically in moving priorities forward at the classroom level, and is not seen as a highly-visible presence around the school. The balance of his/her time appears to many staff to be given over to administration, rather than issues to do with pupils' learning and attainment. He/she does not appear to others as having a clear focus on learning.
		• relationships with people and development of teamwork	3	He/she has very good relationships with staff, pupils and parents. Some good teams have been set up. SMT teamwork is generally seen as very strong. Many see the headteacher as needing to encourage and support more people to become involved in school working groups. The lack of a clear structure for self-evaluation means that good practice is not always identified, celebrated and disseminated effectively.
2.2 3.3	Other selected PIs and themes (see page 10)	• overall quality of attainment • meeting pupils' needs	2	Department or stage audits for the development plan indicate a number of areas where the overall evaluation of these PIs was only fair.

4.3 Exemplar C: A Plan for a Closer Look at Leadership [Anytown School]

Anytown School opted to follow up the **broad view** of the headteacher's leadership and to focus on **Theme 2: Leadership qualities of the headteacher** because it was given a Level 2 award. The headteacher asked his/her depute to manage this **closer look** exercise, consider further sources of evidence and identify in detail some areas for improvement.

The plan set out below uses **PI 7.4** and the **ten key characteristics of effective leadership** to:

i)   agree a set of questions
ii)   identify the features of very good performance drawing on the Level 4 illustrations, the ten key characteristics and the criteria in Appendix 3
iii) agree ways to find out how close the headteacher is to these levels of performance.

Performance Indicator 7.4: Effectiveness of Leadership; Theme 2: Leadership qualities of the headteacher

How do you know?	Some features you might look for (what would "very good" look like?)	How would you find out?
How wide a range of relevant interpersonal skills does the headteacher demonstrate? How well is the headteacher developing personal credibility in the school community?	• Has professional integrity and is confident and reliable • Is a good motivator, communicator and listener • Stimulates people's imagination about what can be achieved • Acknowledges and supports good work and achievements • Staff, pupils and parents are positive about their interaction with the headteacher • Demonstrates effective professional expertise in day-to-day work • Is a source of information and advice on educational practice	• Surveys and questionnaires specific to leadership • Discussion with staff, pupils or parents • Evidence from headteacher review process and report
To what extent is the headteacher a positive influence on the school? To what extent has the headteacher demonstrated commitment and purpose in his/her work?	• Regular opportunities are provided for staff discussion and debate • The headteacher provides the energy and drive to get things done • Staff respond positively and creatively to new initiatives • There is a strong commitment in the school to key priorities such as improving learning and teaching and pupils' attainment • People exhibit a strong commitment to high standards in all aspects of the work of the school	• Analysis of processes of school development • Extent of implementation and evaluation of the school development plan • Analysis of composition of teams and working groups

How do you know?	Some features you might look for (what would "very good" look like?)	How would you find out?
How aware is the headteacher of the school's strengths and areas requiring improvement? To what extent does the headteacher delegate appropriately to develop teamwork?	• Staff and pupils are encouraged to be reflective, set realistic but challenging targets, agree strategies for overtaking these and engage in productive review • The headteacher ensures through personal involvement and effective organisation that a full and accurate picture of the school's work is available across all key areas • There is delegation of challenging and rewarding tasks • The headteacher gives a high priority to building confidence and self-esteem in others and helping colleagues to develop • Staff feel part of a team and contribute to school planning and policy making	• Information from annual reviews • Evidence of a formal and systematic approach to self-evaluation and headteacher's particular contribution • Analysis of staff development and review process
To what extent does the headteacher provide a clear vision and direction for the school that leads to effective learning and teaching? To what extent is the headteacher responsive to the views of others?	• Clear sense of purpose which commands wide support • Clear about own educational values • Short and medium-range targets are set for the school • Appropriate aims have been agreed and staff, pupils and parents have been involved in the process. Prominence is given to the agreed aims. • Headteacher communicates openly with staff and provides reasons for making decisions which are rational and fair • Decisions demonstrate flexibility and creativity but with an uncompromising stance on standards and quality	• Analysis of how aims are used in planning and evaluation • Discussion with staff about ownership of aims • Existence of action plans related to issues arising from monitoring and evaluation
To what extent does the headteacher demonstrate commitment to continuous improvement? How responsive is the headteacher to the views of other stakeholders?	• Clear strategies to promote continuous improvement • Personal involvement in evaluating, planning and implementing improvements • Effective joint activities with other schools and community groups • Strong recognition of the part played by individuals and groups outside the school	• Analysis of school development plan • Activities, records and outcomes of meetings • Discussions with surveys of views of other stakeholders • School calendar of events involving wider community; newsletters

4.4 Exemplar D: Summing Up the Results [Anytown School]

Using the plan for a **closer look**, Anytown School collected a range of evidence on the headteacher's leadership and summarised the key findings. This **closer look** at the selected theme was used to confirm or amend the earlier evaluation in the **broad view** and at the same time highlighted strengths and areas for improvement.

Although the overall evaluation of this theme confirmed the PI Level 2 awarded in the **broad view**, much more information about the headteacher's leadership was acquired to assist in the planning for further improvement. This summary evaluation subsequently contributed to the section on Leadership and Management in Anytown School's Standards and Quality Report.

Performance Indicator 7.4: Effectiveness of Leadership
Theme 2: Leadership qualities of the headteacher
Summary Evaluation
The survey of staff and School Board opinion showed that all respondents felt the headteacher was very approachable and available, and someone who created confidence. The ability to take difficult decisions and make the reasons clear to all involved was a strength commented on by many.   The headteacher shows very strong personal commitment, but he/she is perceived as lacking a clear strategy and overall focus on learning and teaching. Staff feel that some recent priorities have not been taken forward purposefully. Evidence of regular monitoring and review of progress and of the headteacher's 'hands on' involvement is limited.   Analysis of the composition of working groups over the past two years shows that only about 35% of staff have been involved.   The headteacher's own review confirmed that he/she had a clear vision for the school. However, most staff felt the vision had not been shared effectively with them or with pupils. The school aims had not been reviewed for seven years. None of the school policy statements and development plans demonstrates clear links with these aims or the overall vision for school improvement.   A strong feature of the headteacher's leadership is the well-planned procedures to track and review pupil attainment involving all staff. However, limited use is made of up-to-date analyses of attainment to promote further improvement. Sixty per cent of staff have been reviewed. A concentration on day-to-day events by the headteacher had resulted in the postponements of two reviews of SMT colleagues which, in turn, resulted in delays to the reviews of others.

Overall Evaluation	
Clear strengths in some areas of headship but some important weaknesses in significant aspects of leadership.	2

4.5 Exemplar E: Identifying Improvements [Anytown School]

The headteacher of Anytown School found it helpful to separate improvements related to his/her **personal** development from those which related to the **school** as a whole.

A further useful approach was to consider action in both these categories in terms of:

- things to stop doing
- things to keep doing
- things to start doing.

Action required	
School **1. Things to stop doing** • allowing events to interfere with reviews • tending to involve the same staff in working groups. **2. Things to keep doing** • being approachable and available • explaining reasons for decisions taken • continuing the focus on attainment. **3. Things to start doing** • launch a review of school aims and begin to develop a shared vision • demonstrate a clearer focus on learning • increase the level of classroom observation and monitoring • be more systematic about evaluating improvements and development priorities • make more effective use of attainment data to promote improvement.	**Personal** **1. Things to stop doing** • focusing too much on day-to-day events • administrative tasks others can do. **2. Things to keep doing** • using a range of leadership styles • sharing the reasons for decisions. **3. Things to start doing** • find a headteacher colleague to act as a critical friend; arrange visits to each other's schools • in-service/find ways of improving time management.

4.6 Exemplar F: Taking Action for Improvement [Anytown School]

4.6.1 'School' Action Points

The headteacher, after consultation, has given priority to one of the 'school' action points because it will increase the focus on learning and have most impact on pupil attainment. It will also raise the headteacher's and SMT profile in relation to learning and teaching. The action plan which is set out below now forms part of the school development plan.

Priority Area:	Learning and Teaching		PIs 3.1, 3.2, 3.3, 3.4
Purpose:	To improve the quality of pupils' learning experiences and raise attainment by focusing on monitoring the quality of learning and teaching in S1/2 in Year 1, S3/4 in Year 2 and S5/6 in Year 3 as part of the school's three-year strategic plan		
Targets	**Implementation strategies**	**Timescale**	**Resource requirements**	**Success criteria**

Targets	Implementation strategies	Timescale	Resource requirements	Success criteria
HT to take lead responsibility for improving the quality of pupils' learning experiences and significantly raising levels of attainment by Year 3 by engaging the HT and members of the SMT in undertaking observation of S1/2 classes in Year 1, S3/4 classes in Year 2 and S5/6 in Year 3. The focus of class visits to be: • the quality of the teaching process • the quality of pupils' learning • meeting pupils' needs • the use of assessment as part of teaching.	• Learning and teaching group, in consultation with HT, SMT and staff, to agree the focus for monitoring the quality of pupils' learning experiences using PIs 3.1, 3.2, 3.3 and 3.4 for *How good is our school?* and produce common format for recording observations. • In liaison with relevant PT, HT and other members of SMT to arrange a timetable of a minimum of three visits to S1/2 classes in each linked department by December. • HT to report on the progress of task at SMT and PT meetings against timescales, resource requirements and success criteria outlined in the action plan. • Evaluation of impact of initiative to form a part of departmental quality reviews in May among HT, PT and link member of SMT and to be incorporated into department action plans by Year 2.	**Year 1** • **By September** – programme of visits and common format for recording observations developed. • **By December** – classroom visits and class shadowing complete and departments given feedback on observations. • **By June** – school considers findings at an in-service day. Departments to include implementation of key recommendations in development plans for Year 2. • **Years 2-3** – extend practice to S3/4 and S5/6, including peer observation and HT shadowing, as part of the school's three-year strategic plan.	Allocation of time in INSET, PAT and DMs. • **August INSET** – introduce and clarify the initiative. HT to lead. • **September** – meeting of Learning and Teaching group in PAT to agree common format for recording observations. DM time to agree programme of visits. • **September/ December** – HT and SMT to visit relevant classes. HT and SMT to shadow S1 and S2 classes and prepare feedback.	• All departments will have identified strengths and areas for development to improve the quality of pupils' learning experiences. • Each department will have produced a clear action plan for Year 2 to address issues identified through classroom visiting process. • HT/SMT monitoring is shown to have a positive impact on pupil performance and attainment – see school attainment targets. • SMT seen to have higher profile in monitoring, learning and teaching around the school (as shown by staff survey).

4.6.2 'Self' Action Points

Personal action planning can be done in a variety of ways to suit individual preferences. The headteacher of Anytown School drew up a brief plan to act as an aide-memoire.

Rationale

The headteacher recognised that personal credibility is a key characteristic that he/she should develop further. A concentration on administrative tasks had deflected him/her from having sufficient personal involvement in taking forward changes and improvements, and talking with colleagues about important issues in learning and teaching. He/she believes the help of a headteacher colleague will offer some fresh insights, particularly in how best to communicate a shared-school vision.

Approach

He/she plans to

- approach his/her co-reviewer, a headteacher of a similar-sized school, who has had recent opportunity to observe his/her leadership in the school, to act as a critical friend

- arrange a visit to that headteacher's school to gather evidence from both the headteacher and his/her colleagues about how their personal credibility has been established

- invite the critical friend to meet informally to compare ideas and discuss approaches

- arrange for another visit by the critical friend to his/her school, some months later, to gather evidence from both the headteacher and other colleagues, and evaluate the progress made in establishing personal credibility

- acquire some background and knowledge by reading a number of identified key texts, including those leadership case studies in which personal credibility is considered a key characteristic.

development

prioritising

credibility

communication

5 **⋯⋗** **Evaluating and Improving Leadership in Your Own School**
Staff Development and Self-Evaluation Activities

motivation

teamwork

interpersonal skills

focus

delegating

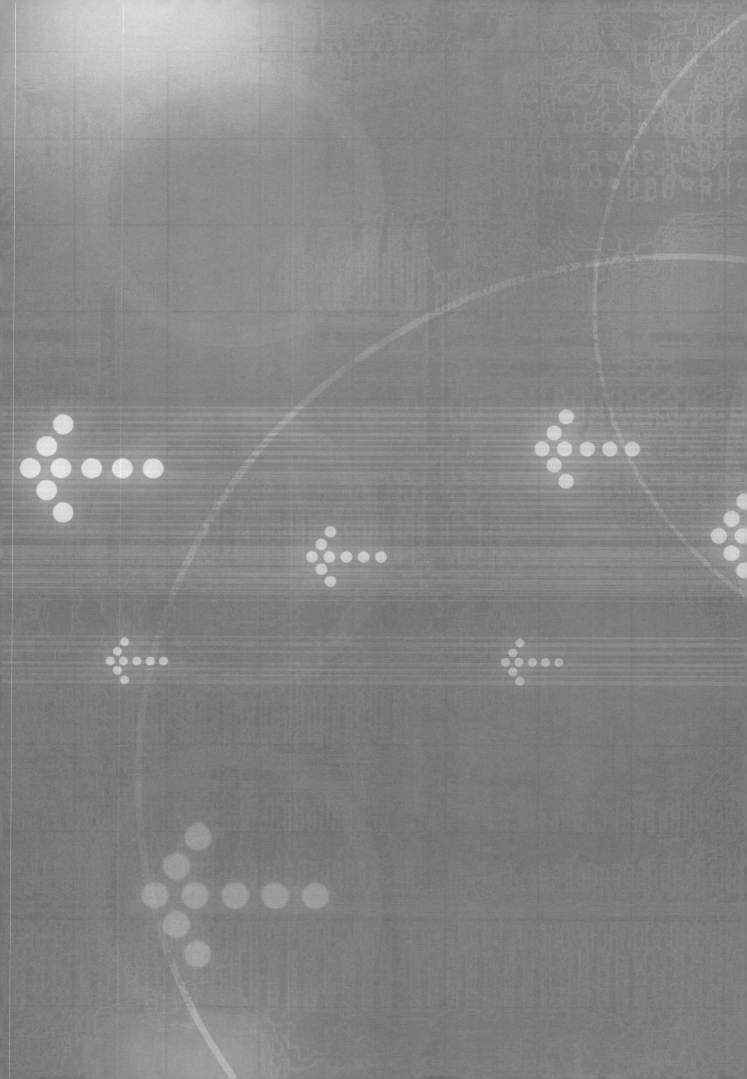

5. Evaluating and Improving Leadership in Your Own School: Staff Development and Self-Evaluation Activities

The previous examples of Anytown School have illustrated key steps in the process of evaluation and improving leadership. In this section, on pages 36-46, you will find similar activities and materials to apply in your own school.

Activity 1: Awareness Raising; What Is an Effective Leader?

Activity 2: Taking a Broad View of Leadership

Activity 3: Taking a Closer Look at Leadership

Activity 4: Summing Up the Results

Activity 5: Identifying Improvements

Activity 6: Taking Action for Improvement

Organising the staff development activities

You may use these activities to consider the effectiveness of leadership at one or more levels in your school. For example, you might decide to consider the leadership of:

- the headteacher
- the senior management team
- a stage or department in a primary or secondary school
- senior teachers.

The activities can be adapted to suit the available staff development time. Although it is important to plan how you are going to evaluate, this should not take up too much time. **As far as possible, you should aim to look for evidence which is available from going about your normal activities, building evaluation in where feasible.** The most important task is to decide what you are going to do with the evidence that you have collected.

Tasks are designed to get you started by encouraging discussion. You should adapt the approaches to suit your circumstances and the resources available. **Your professional judgement is at the heart of the process.** Once begun, you will be on the road to carrying out your evaluation of leadership in your school and to drawing up an appropriate plan of action to bring about any required improvements. As demonstrated in Section 1, such improvements in leadership at various levels in the school have the potential to have a very significant impact on the quality of pupils' learning.

5.1 Activity 1: Awareness Raising; What Is an Effective Leader?

Purpose: To raise awareness of the importance of leadership across the staff and consider the criteria which you would use to judge the effectiveness of leadership at the various levels within the school: headteacher, management team and middle management.

Time: 45 minutes

Task: A In your group, discuss the main characteristics you would value in an effective leader in schools. As a group, agree on five characteristics which you consider to be the key to effective leadership. The criteria from each group can be collected and collated.

B Now look at the ten key characteristics of effective leadership which are listed on page 10 of this document and developed further on pages 12-15. These have been derived from the evidence of inspections and the findings of research. Through discussion, put the ten characteristics into priority order and consider whether any aspects from your group list require to be added. Once again, the findings of the school groups can be discussed and a collated version agreed.

5.2 Activity 2: Taking a Broad View of Leadership

Purpose: To gain a quick impression of the effectiveness of leadership at the selected level within the school.

Time: 45 minutes

Task: This activity asks you to take a broad look at leadership individually or collectively as a team. A blank grid for this activity is provided on page 38, and you should refer to Exemplar B, Anytown School on page 26.

Performance Indicator 7.4 - Effectiveness of Leadership

There is one indicator in *How good is our school?* which focuses directly on leadership, PI 7.4. It can be used as the starting point for taking a **broad view.** (The extended guidance on PI 7.4 which was issued to education authorities in 1999 is included at Appendix 3, Page 62.)

The performance indicator is concerned with the following themes:

- professional competence and commitment
- leadership qualities
- relationships with people and development of teamwork.

It refers to the headteacher of a primary, secondary or special school, the head of a secondary department or others with leadership responsibilities.

Use of other PIs

Although PI 7.4 refers specifically to Effectiveness of Leadership, other indicators will contribute to making decisions of the quality of the leadership at the various levels within the school. Particularly relevant PIs are: 1.1 Quality of the curriculum; 2.3 Overall quality of attainment; 3.1 Quality of the teaching process; 3.2 Quality of pupils' learning; 3.3 Meeting pupils' needs; 5.1 Ethos; 7.1 Self-evaluation; 7.2 The development plan; 7.3 Implementing the development plan. Unless all of these are evaluated at Level 3 or above, or most are 4s, it would be difficult to justify an overall award of 4 for leadership in Performance Indicator 7.4. If several are evaluated at Levels 2 or 1, it would be difficult to justify an overall award of 3 for leadership.

Use of survey questionnaires

The quality of the evaluation will be improved if the views of others can be ascertained through a survey. This need not be time consuming. An example is provided in Appendix 2 on Page 61. The illustrations in PI 7.4, together with the ten key characteristics of effective leadership, have been used to construct this instrument.

5.2 Activity 2 (Blank Grid): Taking a Broad View of Leadership Using PI 7.4, the Ten Characteristics of Effective Leadership and Other Related PIs

Complete the PI grid below for each of the three themes listed for PI 7.4, assigning one of the four levels to each of the themes and to any other appropriate indicators which you agree have a contribution to evaluation of leadership.

4 = very good (major strengths); 3 = good (strengths outweigh weaknesses); 2 = fair (some important weaknesses); 1 = unsatisfactory (major weaknesses)

To help with your decision-making, you should note any areas or aspects of the evidence you have gathered which were important in making your judgement of the level.

Person/Team to whom the evaluation refers

	Management, Leadership & Quality Assurance	Performance Indicator Theme	Level	Evidence to make this judgement
7.4	Effectiveness of leadership	• professional competence and commitment		
		• leadership qualities		
		• relationships with people and development of teamwork		
	Other related PIs and themes	•		

5.3 Activity 3: Taking a Closer Look at Leadership

This is an optional activity. Some schools will find the range and depth of evidence drawn upon for the **broad view**, and the overall conclusions, sufficient to begin to plan the action for improvement. Other schools may, like Anytown School, wish to take a closer look at leadership performance before planning action.

This activity is in two parts. A blank grid for this purpose is on page 41.

i) Describing "very good" performance as a prelude to evaluation

Purpose: To decide what to look for in evaluating present performance in relation to PI 7.4 Effectiveness of Leadership.

In other words, if performance in leadership is "very good", what will it look like? What features might you look for, taking particular account of the ten key characteristics of effective leadership?

Time: 60 minutes

Task: Working as a group, set out the **questions** you would ask and the **features you might look for** to make an evaluation of particular aspects of leadership in your school.

You should consider which specific aspect(s) of leadership you wish to look at, as well as identifying whose leadership is to be evaluated. For example, you could choose to focus on:

- the professional competence and commitment of the management team

- the relationships with people and development of teamwork of the middle managers in the school

- any of the three themes from PI 7.4 and apply these to an individual or a team.

For the chosen theme or themes, use the illustration at Level 4 (*How good is our school?*, page 67), the new extended guidance on PI 7.4 (Appendix 3) and the ten key characteristics of effective leadership to create a set of questions to answer the question "how do you know?". The questions may be set out as pairs as in the worked example for the headteacher of Anytown School (Exemplar C) on page 27.

For each pair of questions, list the main features of good practice. These features can be identified by discussion and reference to such sources as:

- the illustrations in *How good is our school?* (page 67)
- the ten key characteristics of effective leadership
- *Effective Primary Schools* and *Effective Secondary Schools*
- The Standard for Headship in Scotland
- Appendix 3; Advice on Performance Indicator 7.4 Effectiveness of Leadership (Issued to Education Authorities in 1999) (page 62)
- Appendix 4; How Well is the School Led; Senior Management Team (page 63).

ii) How do we know? How would we find out? Identifying the methods we will use to find out

Purpose: To identify the methods which will be used for collecting evidence

Time: 45 minutes

Task: Once the description of "very good" (Level 4) practice has been agreed, proceed to identify which methods you will use to find out how good the practice is in your own school.

There are a number of ways in which you might find evidence, for example:

- talking with individuals and groups
- questionnaires
- checklists
- observation
- looking at documentation
- examining pupils' work
- analysing pupils' progress and performance.

Again consider the approach illustrated in the worked example from Anytown School Exemplar C on page 27.

Often you will be able to use one method (e.g. a questionnaire) to cover a number of key questions related to leadership, as the exemplar for Anytown School shows. As far as possible you should try to save time **by using existing evidence and procedures** such as minutes of meetings, the development plan and annual review processes.

5.3 Activity 3 (Blank Grid): Taking A Closer Look at Leadership: Describing "very good performance" and how we would find out

Performance Indicator 7.4: Effectiveness of Leadership ....

Theme: ....

Consider the above theme. For the theme, use the illustration at Level 4 of *How good is our school?* and the ten key characteristics of effective leadership to:

a) complete a set of questions to help you answer, *how do you know?*
b) set out the main features of good practice and then identify possible sources of evidence for evaluation.

How do you know?	Features you might look for (What would "very good" look like?)	How would you find out?

5.4 Activity 4: Summing Up the Results

Purpose: To sum up your final evaluation and the evidence you have found so that you can plan what you are going to do next.

Time: 45 - 60 minutes

Task: Exemplar D on page 29 shows a summary of the results from Anytown School. Use the blank grid provided on page 43 to sum up in a similar way the main conclusions of your evaluation of the aspect you selected in activity 2 for your own school. This summary should reflect both quality and quantity.

Performance Indicator 7.4: Effectiveness of Leadership of ....

Theme: ....

Summary Evaluation

Overall Evaluation	Level

5.5 Activity 5: Identifying Improvements

Purpose: To use the summary of your evidence and your overall evaluation to identify and plan what you are going to do next.

Time: 30 minutes

Task: Exemplar E from Anytown School on page 30 shows a summary of the action points using the approach,

- what shall I stop doing?
- what shall I keep doing?
- what shall I start doing?

Use the blank grid provided on page 45 to sum up in a similar way the main action points both for your school and yourself.

'**School**' action points are those which will be included as targets in the school development plan. '**Personal**' includes action points for individual action plans. Several staff may be involved in drawing up their own personal action plans, depending on the aspect of school leadership which has been reviewed.

As illustrated in the summary of the overall process on page 22, when planning action for improvement it will be helpful to refer to some of the case studies of effective leadership on pages 67-113.

5.5 Activity 5 (Blank Grid): Identifying Improvements

Action required: a) School b) Personal	
a) School 1. Things to stop doing 2. Things to keep doing 3. Things to start doing	b) Personal 1. Things to stop doing 2. Things to keep doing 3. Things to start doing

5.6 Activity 6: Taking Action for Improvement

Purpose: To use the results of your evaluation and identification of improvements to create an action plan.

Time: 45 minutes

Task: Now that you have summed up the results of your evaluation, and considered the action points, what adjustments do you make to the targets in your school development plan, to reflect the 'school' action points in particular?

In Exemplar F for Anytown School on page 31 there is an example of an action plan. You will wish to develop similar action plan/s using your school's own approach to action planning.

When considering the action plan arising from this activity, you should take particular care to make the targets for improvement **SMART:**

- Specific
- Measurable
- Attainable
- Relevant
- Time-limited.

Your action plan should also show:

- who is responsible for managing the implementation
- what will be done
- the order in which things will be done
- who will do them
- the timescale for carrying them out
- success criteria
- resources and staff development
- how progress will be monitored and evaluated, including PIs to be used.

development

prioritising

credibility

communication

6 ⋯⋗ **Appendices**

motivation

teamwork

interpersonal skills

focus

delegating

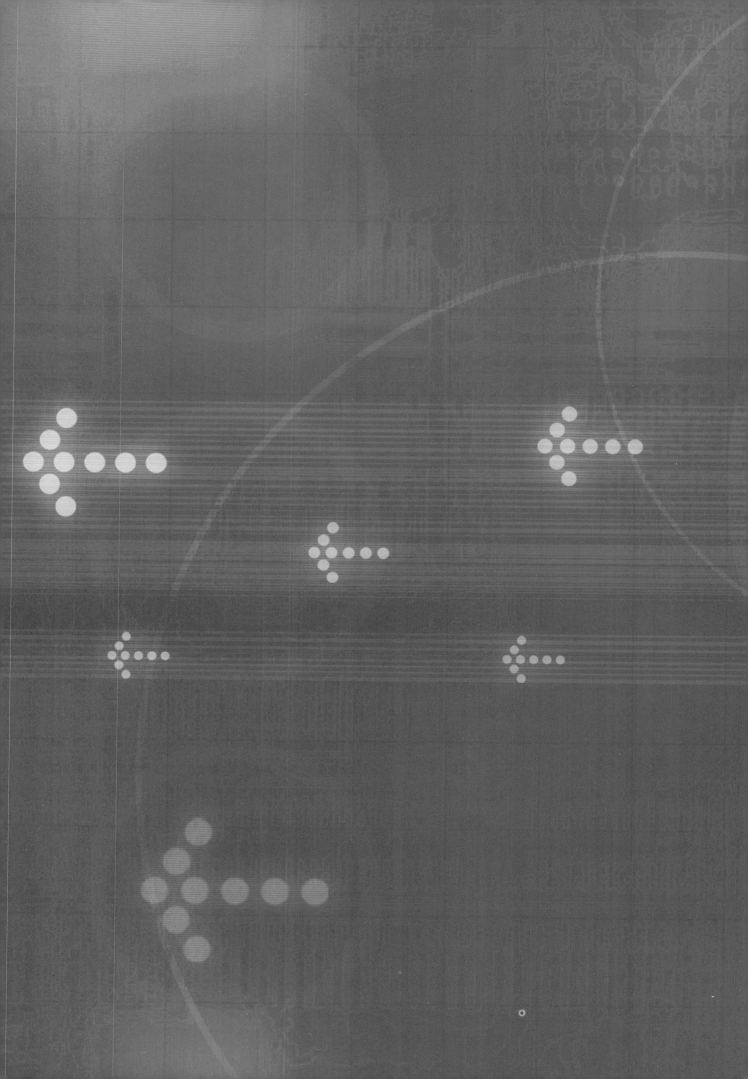

Appendix 1

Ten Characteristics of Effective Leadership - set of slides

Leadership

(a set of slides for introducing staff development activities on leadership)

Ten Characteristics of Effective Leadership

- Building alliances within and beyond the school

- Being committed and purposeful

- Developing teamwork

- Developing and sharing a vision

- Focusing on learning

- Demonstrating interpersonal skills

- Developing personal credibility

- Prioritising

- Being responsive

- Delegating and sharing leadership

Building alliances within and beyond the school

- Understanding the context of their schools and systematically seeking out and developing productive partnerships in the immediate and wider community

- Recognising the need for support, challenge and stimulation through encouraging the observations of others who are external to the school

- Setting out to create networks for the support and improvement of the school

- Working in partnership with pupils, parents and staff

Being committed and purposeful

- Having a clear sense of purpose which commands wide support

- Energy and drive inspiring others to get things done

- Proactive in identifying areas for improvement

- Strong personal commitment to key priorities such as improving learning and teaching and pupil attainment

- Encouraging and motivating in approach to ensure that all are committed to working towards high pupil attainment

- Strong commitment to high standards in all aspects of school work

- Drive and commitment inspiring and motivating others to give of their best

- Being careful to share purpose with others and to build wide support

Developing teamwork

- Building effective teams

- Identifying and developing everybody's potential

- Selecting and developing staff in the knowledge of their complementary, as well as their individual, strengths

- Using conflicts of views constructively to promote professional growth and to negotiate a revised consensus on the way forward

Developing and sharing a vision

- Looking beyond the present and helping others to embrace a strategic educational vision of the future

- Vision taking appropriate account of the views and needs of a range of stakeholders on the school community

- Planning collaboratively to make the vision a reality by setting short and medium-term targets

- Being prepared for, and welcome, the unexpected

- Being clear of purpose, beliefs and values and what is the core of the work and practice

- Being clear of the context in which they work and how to translate national and council agendas into action

- Communicating openly with staff and providing reasons for making decisions which are rational and fair

Focusing on learning

- Recognising pupils' learning as his/her 'core business'

- Putting learning at the centre of the school/dept's activities

- Encouraging talk about learning

- Promoting a climate of evaluation and enquiry

- Encouraging learning and development at every level

- Modelling learning and development themselves

- People regularly talking about improving pupil progress

- Teachers as learners working individually and together

Demonstrating interpersonal skills

- Understanding self - strengths and weaknesses - and are consistent
- Understanding issues from the point of view of others
- Good motivator and can inspire others
- Good communicator and listener
- Confident and reliable in their role
- Clear about own beliefs, values and educational philosophy
- Giving high priority to building confidence and self-esteem in others
- Accentuating the positive, provide praise and encouragement
- Defusing potential problems and conflict

Developing personal credibility

- Professional expertise in day-to-day work
- Source of information and advice on educational practice
- Providing encouragement and support
- Being persuasive and providing 'hands-on' leadership
- Understanding school, local and national context
- Having a capacity to translate aims into reality
- Gaining the trust of staff through knowledge, expertise, commitment and working practice
- Having time for people and valuing their work and their views
- Model of good practice for the staff and the school community
- Modelling a commitment to school improvement

Prioritising

- Being clear about what matters most
- Agreeing targets
- Being clear about where their time will be used to best effect
- Prominence being given to agreed aims
- Day-to-day practice reflecting their strategic priorities in action
- The key objectives of the school are discussed, shared and influence practice
- Promoting understanding of the key issues
- Staff respond positively and creatively to new initiatives

Being responsive

- Listening carefully to pupils, staff, parents and the wider community

- Keeping closely in touch with emerging issues and needs

- Responding flexibly and creatively but with an uncompromising stance on standards and quality

- Valuing difference – managing conflict creatively as a way to getting different views

- Welcoming challenges to existing practice and conformity

- Openness to participation in debate

- Seeking to understand before making judgements

Delegating and sharing leadership

- Delegating effectively and positively by recognising strengths and development needs of others

- Creating freedom for focusing leadership on learning and teaching by delegating and streamlining subsidiary administrative tasks

- Using every opportunity to allow others to exercise leadership

- Knowing when to lead and when to follow the lead of others who have evident strengths in particular areas

- Inspiring and empowering staff to make a difference

- Creating leadership opportunities for promoted and unpromoted staff

- Encouraging and supporting people to become involved

60

Appendix 2

Survey of Opinion on Leadership

PI 7.4: Effectiveness of Leadership - using the PI themes, illustrations, and the ten characteristics of effective leadership

Effectiveness Of Leadership	4	3	2	1
• professional competence and commitment				
demonstrates strong personal commitment to key priorities				
day-to-day practice reflects strategic priorities in action				
initiates and manages change in line with vision				
helps others to embrace a strategic educational vision				
provides an effective professional example				
is a source of information and advice on educational practice				
demonstrates a practical ability to translate aims into reality				
promotes a climate of evaluation and enquiry				
recognises pupils' learning and attainment as his/her 'core business'				
• leadership qualities				
creates confidence in others through support and personal example				
inspires and motivates others towards highest expectations				
is approachable and available				
is responsive and a good listener				
provides 'hands-on' leadership which has a positive impact on practice				
commitment, has the energy and drive to get things done				
demonstrates good communication skills				
• relationships with people and development of teamwork				
maintains positive relationships with staff, pupils and parents				
uses every opportunity to allow others to exercise leadership				
recognises the various strengths of others and builds effective teams				
involves others in developing school policies and the school plan				
encourages and supports people to become involved				
seeks out and develops productive partnerships				
delegates effectively and productively to manage change				

Key Area: Management, leadership and quality assurance
Performance Indicator 7.4: Effectiveness of Leadership

Further Advice On PI 7.4 Issued To Education Authorities In 1999

This advice applies to a headteacher's leadership of a school and a principal teacher's or section leader's leadership of a team. In making decisions about leadership, account needs to be taken of the context for leadership; some schools/teams will be more difficult to lead than others. Care should be taken to distinguish leadership skills from more general day-to-day management and administration. Indicators of effective leadership are most likely to include a sense of educational vision, strategic direction, inspiring others through example, effective delegation and teamwork, effective management of change and the promotion of high expectations.

On the assumption that the leader has been in post for several years, direct responsibility for the quality of provision across the seven Key Areas should be reflected in the level awarded for this PI. Particularly relevant PIs are: 1.1 Structure of the curriculum, 2.3 Overall quality of attainment, 3.2 Quality of pupils' learning, 3.3 Meeting pupils' needs, 5.1 Ethos, 7.1 Self-evaluation, 7.2 The development plan, 7.3 Implementing the development plan. Unless all of these are good or better, it would be difficult to justify leadership being very good. If several are fair or unsatisfactory, it would be difficult to justify leadership being good.

How do you know?	Some features you might look for
Does the leader apply his/her knowledge and skills to provide a clear strategic direction to the school/team?	Education philosophy underpinning school's/team's aims is manifestly developed by the leader, shared with staff and applied in classrooms and generally.
Does the leader initiate and manage effective change in the work of the school/team as part of a broader educational vision?	Successful planning processes advance identified priorities in line with a broad strategic view of where the school/team is going.
Does the leader provide a clear example to others including, where applicable, teaching which is a model of good practice?	Leader's commitment and enthusiasm inspires others.
Does the leader inspire and encourage staff to work towards the highest expectations?	Staff are highly motivated to improving pupil attainment in a positive learning environment.
Is the leader fully aware of the school's/team's strengths and areas requiring improvement?	Leader ensures, through personal involvement and effective organisation, that an objective picture of the school's/team's work is available across all key areas.
Does the leader recognise the strengths of staff and take steps to help all to contribute fully and appropriately to the work of the school/team?	Leader makes effective arrangements to be aware of the contribution of each member of staff and to encourage teamwork and staff development.
Does the leader initiate and manage change well? Are innovative ideas and practice promoted and recognised?	In the case of headteachers, he/she interacts with, and deploys, senior promoted staff effectively in dealing with general school management and in managing change.
	Evidence of promotion within the school/team of good practice identified within school/team and more widely.
Is the leader approachable and available?	Staff, parents and pupils are positive about their interactions with the leader.
Does the leader ensure that staff, pupils and parents are fully informed about the work of the school/team?	Staff, pupils and parents get the information they need in an accessible form.
Does the leader ensure that effective delegation and teamwork are widely promoted in the school/team?	Leader delegates tasks to make the best use of the strengths of staff. Staff feel part of a team.
Does policy development and planning involve staff sufficiently and ensure commitment to the agreed outcomes?	Staff contribute well to developing school/team policies and the school plan and to taking them forward.

06

Appendix 4

Example of Performance Indicator 7.4

How Well Is the School Led?; Senior Management Team

This PI is concerned with the following aspects:

- professional competence and commitment
- leadership qualities
- relationship with people and development of teamwork.

How do you know?	Some features you might look for
Do senior staff demonstrate an awareness of, and a commitment to, the processes of self-evaluation? Do senior staff have a grasp of the wider context governing educational change? Do senior staff initiate and manage projects? Is there a commitment to project development?	• Senior staff provide clear and effective leadership in procedures for self-evaluation and quality assurance throughout the school. • Senior staff are knowledgeable about the context in which educational change is taking place. • Senior staff use effective strategies and techniques for managing change. • Senior team meetings are focused, productive and characterised by discussion, debate and clear action. • Senior staff are fully involved in leading and supporting project development.
Is there a commitment to school improvement, school effectiveness and the management of change? Do senior staff encourage the development of innovative and creative projects?	• Senior staff demonstrate a strong commitment to school improvement. • Regular opportunities are provided for staff discussion and debate and the celebration of success. • There are transparent examples of projects which lead to improvement in whole-school, departmental and/or individual effectiveness. • Senior staff help the school to learn from successes as well as mistakes.
Do senior staff provide clear strategies for improving performance – their own, staff and pupils?	• Senior staff assist teachers to select appropriate tools and techniques for improvement. • There are good opportunities for staff development linked to agreed priorities. • Staff and pupils are encouraged to be reflective, to set realistic but challenging targets and to agree effective strategies for overtaking these.

How do you know?	Some features you might look for
Do senior staff raise awareness of the need for culture change?	• Senior staff share a vision for school improvement and present change positively. • Staff are encouraged to see themselves as the key resources, managers of learning, team leaders and co-ordinators of projects. • Staff have effective techniques for managing change effectively. • Staff develop and maintain positive attitudes. • Senior staff use good interpersonal skills and techniques to overcome barriers to change.
Do senior staff articulate and work to values and vision? Do they provide a clear direction for the school which leads to effective learning and teaching?	• Senior staff are highly visible around the school and good role models. • Senior staff are persuasive and provide 'hands on' leadership.
Do senior staff show confidence and courage when confronting difficult issues?	• Senior staff do not avoid difficult issues, communicate openly with staff and provide reasons for making decisions which are rational and fair. • Staff feel they are consulted about important decisions. • Working relationships are characterised by a shared sense of purpose and a willingness to negotiate.
Do senior staff value and promote teamworking?	• Staff are provided with a range of opportunities to work in teams and to reflect on their team skills. • There is evidence of different types of groups for different purposes. • Staff are skilled in groupwork.
Do senior staff create a climate which develops the expertise and enthusiasm of staff and others in the wider school community?	• Senior staff regularly encourage staff and pupils to share a sense of ownership and show commitment to the school. • There is a positive and encouraging atmosphere about the school. • Evidence of collaborative ventures and strategies demonstrates the capacity of parents, teachers and the wider community to work together.
Do senior staff encourage all members of the community to contribute to feedback on the effectiveness of the school?	• The school regularly provides high quality information on its work and effectiveness. • Members of the community feel well informed about the work of the school and have good opportunities to make comment.

development

prioritising

credibility

communication

7 ···> Case Studies - Leadership in Action

motivation

teamwork

interpersonal skills

focus

delegating

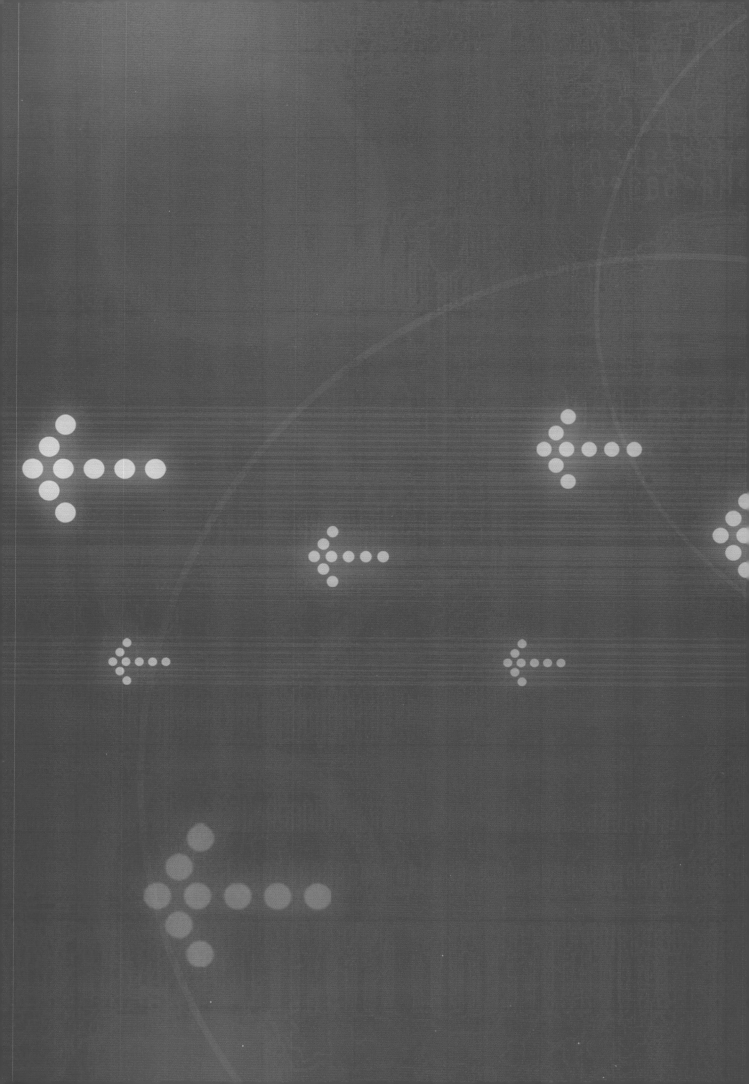

7. Case Studies – Leadership in Action

This section presents a number of case studies of effective school leadership in a range of contexts. **Four full case studies of schools outline the key characteristics of leadership in some detail. A further ten school case studies focus on each of the key leadership characteristics.** All the case study schools were schools in which recent inspections by HMI had identified high quality leadership skills in operation. The case studies focus on particular skills which were exemplified for purposes of illustration. The highlighting of any one particular leadership characteristic in a case study school does not imply that others were not present too. In practice, leadership in each of the case study schools covered many of the ten key characteristics and the written account has been deliberately selective.

Many of the case studies focus on the leadership of headteachers as a key feature in school improvement. In addition, there are examples of effective leadership being provided by depute headteachers and principal teachers. **Two separate case studies focus on the steps taken by individual teachers to improve their own leadership skills through the Scottish Qualification for Headship.**

Overall, the case studies are intended to show the key characteristics of leadership at work in real schools and the way in which such leadership skills can and should be developed at all levels of the school organisation. **The case studies are intended to be used selectively in association with appropriate staff development activities such as those provided on page 69.** The grid on page 71 provides a convenient way of identifying the particular leadership characteristics considered in each of the case study schools.

School	Focus of the Case Study
Full Case Studies	
1. Isobel Mair School East Renfrewshire Council	Leadership in learning and child development
2. Clackmannan Primary School Clackmannanshire Council	Leadership to turn a school around
3. Larkhall Academy South Lanarkshire Council	Leadership to improve a school's image
4. Moffat Academy Dumfries & Galloway Council	Leadership to improve learning and teaching
Case Studies Exemplifying Each of the Ten Characteristics	
5. Seafield Infant School West Lothian Council	Leadership and quality assurance
6. Auchenlodment Primary School Renfrewshire Council	Leadership and teamwork
7. Kingswells Primary School Aberdeen City Council	Leadership to raise attainment in English language and mathematics
8. Laxdale Primary School Comhairle nan Eilean Siar	Leadership for continuous improvement
9. Lochside Primary School Angus Council	Leadership and staff self-evaluation
10. Balfron High School Stirling Council	Leadership focused on improving subject examination performance
11. Banff Academy Aberdeenshire Council	Leadership to promote teamwork
12. Bannerman High School Glasgow City Council	Leadership to develop co-operation among staff
13. Larbert High School Falkirk Council	Leadership to promote an ethos of achievement
14. Webster's High School Angus Council	Leadership to develop primary-secondary liaison
Training in Leadership and Management	
15. Scottish Qualification for Headship	Depute headteacher, Edinburgh City Council
16. Scottish Qualification for Headship	Headteacher, Glasgow City Council

Leadership Case Studies - Staff Development Activities

The case studies can be used to assist staff development in leadership in many ways. The activities set out below are only some of the possibilities which are suitable for individuals or small groups.

Activity 1

Purpose: To analyse, using different case studies, how a particular leadership characteristic is exercised

Time: 30 - 60 minutes

Task: Choose a leadership characteristic that you would like to explore in more detail. From the case studies/leadership characteristics grid (page 71), select those case studies in which this particular leadership characteristic is demonstrated. Consider the following questions and make a note of your answers.

What are the common themes in the ways leadership developed in the selected case studies?

What similarities do you find in the approach in these selected case studies? Can you suggest reasons why these similarities exist?

What differences are there in the approaches? Can these be explained solely by the differences in the particular context?

Can you think of examples from your own experience when this particular characteristic was used to good effect?

How do you exercise this particular leadership characteristic in your own role/school? In what respects might you wish to make changes in light of the case study evidence?

Activity 2

Purpose: To explore how leadership is provided within a particular context

Time: 30 - 40 minutes

Task: Choose a case study with a context that matches a key priority in your own school development plan.

Consider answers to the following questions and make a note of your answers.

What marks out the performance of the case study school within this context as very good? What is your evaluation of the performance of your own school within this context?

What was done in the case study school to make the performance very good? What were the key strengths of the approach? Were there any weaknesses?

In light of the case study evidence, are any changes suggested to present and future targets in your school plan?

What leadership characteristics would be important in taking forward a similar development in your own school?

Characteristics Of Leadership : The Case Study Schools

Characteristics Of Leadership	FULL CASE STUDY				CASE STUDIES OF A SINGLE CHARACTERISTIC									
	ISOBEL MAIR SCHOOL	CLACKMANNAN PS	LARKHALL ACADEMY	MOFFAT ACADEMY	SEAFIELD INFANT SCHOOL	AUCHENLODMENT PS	KINGSWELLS PS	LAXDALE PS	LOCHSIDE PS	BALFRON HS	BANFF ACADEMY	BANNERMAN HS	LARBERT HS	WEBSTER'S HS
1. Building alliances within and beyond the school	✓	✓	✓					✓						
2. Being committed and purposeful	✓					✓								
3. Developing teamwork		✓	✓	✓							✓			
4. Developing and sharing a vision	✓		✓										✓	
5. Focusing on learning	✓			✓			✓							
6. Demonstrating interpersonal skills				✓								✓		
7. Developing personal credibility	✓	✓	✓	✓						✓				
8. Prioritising		✓							✓					
9. Being responsive			✓		✓									
10. Delegating and sharing leadership		✓												✓

Case Study 1: Leadership in learning and child development

Isobel Mair School   **East Renfrewshire Council**

Background and context

Isobel Mair School is situated in Clarkston. It is a school for children and young people from ages 5 to 19 with moderate, severe or profound learning difficulties. There are a number of children with a diagnosis of autism or who are placed on the autistic continuum. The headteacher, Catherine MacLeod, has been in post for 17 years since the school opened in 1982. The school roll is 44 and there are 27 educational staff.

Why was learning and child development an important focus for leadership?

The headteacher felt that the main focus for the school had to be on the individual child. A holistic curriculum was seen as the key. She believed that the children should be encouraged to be as independent as possible and that the school needed to have a clear vision of where the pupil might be at age 19, when each left school. All of the work with pupils was put into an educational and learning context, for example, the development of eating and dressing skills were seen as key learning experiences promoting pupils' independence.

The nature of leadership in the school

A recent education authority review of the school highlighted the following aspects:

- a caring, committed and enthusiastic staff
- the knowledge, expertise, vision and leadership of the head
- the good school team where individuals complement each other's skills
- the role model of the assistant headteacher.

Leadership in the school is characterised by:

a)   Developing and sharing a vision

When the school opened in 1982, the head had a clear vision of where she wanted the school to go, but she had completely new staff. The staff and head together discussed and brainstormed ideas about how they would take this vision forward as a team. At the time, there were no national curriculum guidelines for pupils with complex educational needs, so the team began by setting objectives and building up a curricular framework. Putting plans and teaching programmes in writing was new to many staff. All staff were encouraged to share and develop the headteacher's vision of the learning process and consider their own role in setting up the learning environment. Now new initiatives are discussed when they are on the horizon. What will they mean for Isobel Mair School? How can these be shaped and used to help develop further the vision for the school?

b)   Building alliances within and beyond the school

When the school was opened, the head realised that some local residents might be uneasy about having a special school in the neighbourhood. She visited households surrounding the school and explained the nature of the school and its vision. She invited local residents to come in and see the school in operation and to meet the children and the staff. One of those who took up this initial offer still comes in to the school to help on a voluntary basis. Students from a local secondary school also come into Isobel Mair School and work with the children. They are given an induction programme so that they feel part of the team and are at ease with the needs of children in the school. All volunteers go through a similar induction, using cards to explain processes and procedures, so that they can work effectively with the children alongside the staff.

Very close links have now been built up with the local community to enable the school to work in partnership to support the integration and socialisation of the children. Similar productive links have been forged with all of the external agencies that work with the children. The staff from these agencies are seen as key members of the 'teaching teams' for the school's five classes.

c)   Focusing on learning

The school operates in 'teaching teams' which include a teacher as team leader, an instructor, class assistants and external agencies. Teaching strategies are continually discussed on a whole-school basis, led by the headteacher, and within the teaching teams. Teaching is based on the philosophy that the child always succeeds. This is achieved by high-quality planning which breaks larger tasks down into smaller achievable steps. Positive and consistent intervention, open communication and co-operative relationships back this up. Staff professional development is enhanced by rotation around the five learning areas. Behaviour modification strategies are part of the teaching process. Developing an assessment profile and framework for all staff to work in is a key to planning and to the overall focus on the child. The assessment profile is linked to the 5-14 programme, is on computer disk for ease of access and assessment is shared with parents.

d)   Being committed and purposeful

A key aspect of the headteacher's role is keeping staff very positive about their work and keeping morale high. Where there seem to be barriers, she encourages staff to consider other ways of working and to share their difficulties, skills and experience with others.

- The commitment of the staff is manifest in the numerous additional qualifications that they have obtained while working in the school. Staff are keen to develop themselves and see the staff development and career review process as very important.

- Staff are encouraged to be reflective in seeking the most appropriate approaches to learning for each pupil and in promoting pupils' acquisition of skills.

e)   Developing personal credibility

The headteacher teaches alongside other staff if there is a difficult situation or a new curricular technique. She is a very strong professional role model, disseminating teaching skills, and working in teams as a team member.

- The headteacher is seen to be at the forefront of developments in the education of children with complex educational needs. She is always willing to share her knowledge and expertise with the staff.

- Everyone is seen as an important member of the school team. Teachers, instructors, class assistants, special needs auxiliaries, janitor, bus driver, guide and many others are all valued for their contributions to the education of the pupils.

Impact and outcomes of leadership

Staff share a vision for the school that was initially developed through the headteacher's leadership. They constantly help to develop each other professionally. There is a very strong commitment to teamwork and a clear process for professional development of staff. A chart is displayed on the wall of each teaching area showing the developing skills acquisition of staff in specific aspects. The gradings used are 'acquired', 'mastered', 'updated' and 'disseminated'. Other key outcomes of effective leadership have included:

- the school's high reputation locally and nationally, including two Curriculum Awards

- innovative and highly-skilled teaching which focuses on the individual pupil

- regular monitoring and evaluation of the work of the school

- strong partnerships with parents, agencies and associated primary and secondary schools

- a high level of expertise in autism.

How was this leadership developed?

The headteacher developed her interest in learning through reading, research, visiting others and talking to many people in the field of special education. She found the following of particular help:

- continually questioning her practice through self-evaluation
- networking with similar establishments throughout the UK
- taking part in research projects with universities and teacher training colleges
- using critical friends as a means of challenge and support.

Next steps

Future priorities for the headteacher's leadership include:

- formalising the networks with other establishments to share developments
- striving for continuous improvement
- matching learning outcomes for older students to the new framework of National Qualifications.

Case Study 2: Leadership to turn a school around

Clackmannan Primary School   **Clackmannanshire Council**

Background and context

Clackmannan Primary School serves the pupils of the village of Clackmannan and surrounding area. The school has a roll of 335 pupils and 15.3 teachers. The context of this case study is the fundamental and widespread improvement in the school over a period of 20 months following a critical HMI inspection. Progress made by the school within that period, and since, has been notable. The HMI inspection report identified eight main points for action, which included improvements in pupil attainment, staff teamwork, communication, relationships between the headteacher and staff and partnership with parents. The publication of the report in September 1997 was marked by critical press coverage, both national and local, and some strongly-expressed community concerns about the school. The education authority responded very promptly to the report and played a significant part in establishing a culture of improvement in the school by making available some additional staff and other resources and employing the services of a part-time consultant. A new headteacher, Iain Campbell, was appointed to take the process of improvement forward, in close consultation with the education authority.

Why was turning the school around an important focus for leadership?

On taking up appointment, the headteacher knew that the HMI follow-up visit was anticipated within about 18 months. He felt that:

- a rapid improvement in staff teamwork was an essential first step if the main points for action in the HMI report were to be addressed successfully

- helpful preparatory work had been done by the consultant which needed to be built upon

- improved community confidence and support needed to be established quickly for the school to move forward.

The nature of leadership in the school

Since the headteacher's appointment, leadership in the school has been characterised by:

a)   Prioritising

The numerous targets in the school's action plan made prioritising essential. The headteacher discussed and agreed with staff to:

- focus clearly on the curriculum and pupils' attainment with immediate, short-term and long-term priorities

- make reading and mathematics priority areas, with writing to follow soon after

- introduce setting to improve attainment in mathematics at P6/P7.

b)   Developing teamwork

Improved teamwork was a key priority and was developed by:

- agreeing that the senior management would take a lead role in providing starter papers for policy formulation and curriculum development, but that these starter papers would be discussed widely

- setting up staff working groups to encourage staff to take greater responsibility for school development and to work together for improvement

- asking the working groups to develop agreed school policy across a range of issues relating to learning and teaching

- ensuring staff allocation to groups was based both on expressed preferences and the need to bring together teachers who did not normally work together.

c)   Delegating and sharing leadership

The headteacher recognised the need to share leadership with other colleagues in the senior management team and more widely. He did this by:

- delegating specific responsibilities, after consultation, and encouraging senior colleagues to use their initiative

- inviting his deputy to develop her leadership skills in new areas

- delegating leadership responsibilities to a number of other staff through working groups.

d)   Developing personal credibility

The headteacher regularly demonstrated his professional expertise in his day-to-day work by:

- taking the responsibility for drafting key policy documents himself whilst ensuring staff knew about the work being undertaken and sharing all drafts for wider comment and discussion

- accepting many staff suggestions into the revised policies and arranging for all staff to have a folder in which such key documents were filed for easy reference

- meeting with all staff every morning for a five minute discussion of current issues

- agreeing new approaches to forward planning, monitoring the plans regularly and providing detailed feedback

- visiting each class every day to reinforce discipline, acknowledge the achievements of pupils and staff and steadily share his vision of where the school should be.

e)   Building alliances within and beyond the school

The headteacher took the lead in building up good links with parents and the wider community in a number of ways:

- every opportunity was taken to reinforce the key message that the school's senior management welcomed contacts with parents on any issue and accessibility was assured
- a newsletter was sent home each month and parents were encouraged into school at every opportunity to see the changes in ethos for themselves
- the homework policy was revised, shared with parents and a homework club set up
- a number of parents were recruited to assist with a new paired reading scheme
- reports on pupil progress and attainment were revised to provide clearer information to parents
- a positive discipline scheme which was being established was further developed and used to promote a positive ethos and culture within the school.

Impact and outcomes of leadership

The HMI follow-up report confirmed that all of the eight main points for action had been satisfactorily addressed and that the school had made very good overall progress. Working relationships between staff, and between staff and senior management, were now characterised by strong teamwork, mutual trust and a sense of common purpose. Pupils' attainment had increased significantly, especially in mathematics and writing. Setting in mathematics was working well and had significantly improved challenge and differentiation. Parent and community views were now very positive about the school and its future direction.

How was this leadership developed?

The headteacher's leadership developed through:

- reflecting on his own experiences in other schools, including practice he considered had best motivated staff
- developing a vision of the type of school he would like to work in
- developing his skills in communication and staff development as an assistant head in a previous school where he was given significant responsibility for leading a major curriculum development

- recognising the need for 'critical friends' and other colleagues to provide advice, including his own deputy headteacher

- benefiting from the scope given to him by Clackmannanshire Council to set his own approach while making full use of available education authority support

- finding every opportunity to share his views with staff and pupils, particularly through daily visits to each class.

Next steps

The headteacher had used his review meeting to evaluate his progress and identify future priorities.

- A Standards and Quality report will be produced and shared with parents and staff to show how much has been achieved and to highlight future priorities.

- A more consistent approach will be developed to monitoring learning and teaching in order to evaluate the changes which have been made.

- More use will be made of performance indicators in future auditing of school practice.

- A review process will be established with all staff to build upon the improved teamwork and to better prioritise staff development activities.

Case Study 3: Leadership to improve a school's image

Larkhall Academy   **South Lanarkshire Council**

Background and context

Larkhall Academy serves Larkhall and the adjoining villages of Ashgill, Netherburn and Stonehouse. It has a roll of 1,125 and a staffing complement of 77.6 FTE. The headteacher, Tom Dingwall, has been in post for five years. A recent HMI inspection noted the very good leadership of the headteacher who had the respect and confidence of staff, parents and pupils. In his five years in post, he had made improvements to attendance, ethos and the school's overall standing in the community. Senior promoted staff were found to work well together as a team and they provided good support to staff. Principal teachers provided sound leadership to their departments and made a good contribution to the school.

Why was improving the image of the school an important focus for leadership?

At the time of his appointment, staff and the wider community expressed a feeling that there was a low regard for the school in the town. Many pupils and parents were not identifying with the school which was consequently suffering from outward placing requests to other schools. On the positive side, the headteacher recognised the high quality of promoted staff in the school and the commitment of teachers to subject teaching. The focus for the headteacher's initial action was to improve the image of the school amongst staff and pupils and within the wider community.

The nature of leadership in the school

The HMI inspection report noted that the headteacher provided very effective leadership. His leadership in the school includes the following key characteristics:

a)   Developing and sharing a vision

The headteacher had a clear vision to improve the image of the school and to make the staff and the community proud to be identified with it. Shortly after his appointment the members of the senior management team changed. The new team met together for a weekend conference. They discussed the vision for the school and focused on key issues such as, pride in the school, improving relationships with parents and the community and generally raising the confidence and self-esteem. This vision of school improvement was to be translated into reality by:

- recognising the talents of staff and pupils
- meeting all parents to discuss the vision and the way ahead as a team
- discussion with associated primary schools to improve relationships by working together

- developing a rewards and credit system for pupils
- revisiting the vision each year
- moving forward on a new school uniform, although there was an initial negative view from staff as to whether this would be successful.

b)   Building alliances within and beyond the school

The senior management team recognised the need to move forward with the support of the staff and the wider community. The headteacher used his interpersonal skills to try to get others to share the vision. He is a good listener and encouraged parents to express their views about their children's education and the school. The strategy agreed by the senior management team included the following practical steps:

- earlier contact with parents of children in primary school in November of P7 prior to making the choice of secondary school
- senior management team and guidance staff to provide a named person to link with each of the nine associated primary schools
- the link person to attend all primary school parents' evenings (three per year) to talk to parents and build up relationships and trust at an early stage
- the headteacher to attend community meetings and take every opportunity to promote the school and explain the vision
- praising pupils' achievements in the school and wider community
- developing the role of a senior teacher with a remit in external communication to oversee the compilation of regular newspaper reports
- further developing the role of a school magazine celebrating achievements
- holding an award ceremony at an external venue so that parents and the wider community could join in more easily.

c)   Developing teamwork

The new senior management team consisted of senior promoted staff, the resource centre manager and the administrative finance assistant. There was also a Board of Studies that included heads of departments. Policy formulation and developments were now to be taken forward through:

- working groups – each with a clear remit and timescale
- a committee structure with delegated decision-making
- wide consultation and discussion of policy drafts with amendments made based on responses
- staff knowing they will be consulted and be able to influence the outcomes

- introduction of a positive reward scheme, after discussion with staff and pupils, with the procedures displayed on the wall of every classroom. Each department discussed their own approach and criteria for awarding credits and the senior management team visited departmental meetings to ensure consistency of approach across the school.

d)   Developing personal credibility

The headteacher is an excellent role model for the senior management team and staff. He is seen within the school and in the wider community as a person with professional integrity who provides 'hands-on' leadership and gets things done. Some examples of his approach and actions are:

- a willingness to be at the heart of school improvement
- undertaking wide consultation with staff and parents on the school vision and proposed changes
- promoting the wearing of school uniform after discussion with parents
- although staff felt that the proposed wearing of school uniform would be a 'lost cause', they agreed to follow the headteacher's lead: the clear success of the initiative raised the headteacher's credibility and reinforced the vision
- encouraging the persistence of the senior management team in following up requests, checking implementation of policies, monitoring all aspects of school operation and supporting staff
- keeping well informed about new initiatives and being able to communicate to staff the implications for the school
- demonstrating that he was a good motivator and good at working with people.

e)   Being responsive

The headteacher encourages staff to express their opinions, and he has shown that he is comfortable when opinions contrary to his own are expressed. Conflict is used constructively to debate issues, reaching a better solution and sharing the final responsibility for decisions taken. Staff feel that consultation is genuine and recognise it is important to respond to requests for their views. The headteacher's responsiveness is illustrated through:

- supporting individual members of staff and giving freely of his own time
- talking face-to-face with groups of staff or parents to show that the SMT is serious about participation
- being a good listener and interacting confidently with people
- willingly accepting all invitations to speak to groups in the local community and elicit their views about the school

- giving careful consideration to how to respond to difficult situations and, where necessary, taking advice from the education authority.

Impact and outcomes of leadership

As a result of the leadership approaches adopted, the perception of the school has been transformed in the community. School uniform is worn and pupils are happy to identify with the school. Relationships have been improved within the school and the quality of staff meetings and interactions has improved. The school roll is now increasing. Leadership is accepted as important at every level within the organisation. The senior management team is widely recognised as a strength of the school. The school now believes in itself. Pupils and staff have a positive image about Larkhall Academy and themselves. People demonstrate a willingness to go the 'extra mile' in emergencies and pull together in any crisis. The HMI inspection highlighted the following among the school's key strengths:

- partnership with parents and the School Board
- links with the community and the associated primary schools
- management of the learning resources centre
- the quality of personal, social, curricular and vocational guidance.

How was this leadership developed?

Influences on the development of the headteacher's management style included:

- attendance at courses covering various headteacher management training modules
- interaction with other headteachers to debate issues and new initiatives and share good practice
- reading about national and local developments in education and looking in detail at the implications for Larkhall Academy.

Next steps

The headteacher and the school have agreed the following next steps to make further improvements to the school's reputation. Increased focus is planned on:

- raising standards of attainment at all levels
- providing greater challenge for able pupils
- creating quality time to make further improvements in collaborative working
- tracking individual pupil's progress and setting targets for each pupil in S5 and S6
- continuing the developmental focus on learning and teaching
- restructuring the S1/S2 curriculum.

Case Study 4: Leadership to improve learning and teaching

Moffat Academy   **Dumfries and Galloway Council**

Background and context

Moffat Academy serves Moffat, Beattock and the surrounding area. The school has a nursery, primary and secondary department and takes pupils from age 4 to 18. It has a roll of 21 pupils in the nursery, 276 in the primary school and 227 in the secondary. The headteacher, Jeff Brown, has been in post for ten years.

Why was improvement in learning and teaching an important focus for leadership?

'Children are always the only future the human race has. Teach them well'. This statement is framed and hangs outside the headteacher's office. Its message is at the heart of what the school is trying to do. The headteacher continually talks about learning and teaching and encourages this focus among staff across the whole school. He sees this as the 'core business' of a school and points out that having children from age 4 to 18 gives Moffat Academy a key role in shaping young people for the future.

The nature of leadership in the school

The recent HMI inspection of the secondary department of the school noted that:

- the headteacher provided outstanding leadership and had established excellent, positive relationships among staff and pupils

- the headteacher gave a very strong and positive lead which established an excellent atmosphere of high expectations

- the depute headteacher provided effective leadership for a number of initiatives and made a valuable contribution to the day-to-day running of the school

- pupils and staff identified strongly with the school which was highly regarded by parents and enjoyed strong support from its School Board and PTA

- the headteacher, his depute and the many staff who served on working parties or committees contributed very effectively to the management of the school.

Leadership in the school has the following key characteristics:

a)   Focusing on learning

- An external consultant facilitated an INSET day for all staff on 'Teaching for effective learning'.

- Performance indicators for learning and teaching are used across the school, focusing on a stage at a time.

- The headteacher works alongside teachers in classrooms in the nursery, primary and secondary. He regularly teaches classes at all three levels in the school.

- Classroom observation is part of normal practice and is based on clear, agreed criteria. Feedback is detailed and seen to be constructive.

- The school also focuses on the teacher as a learner, developing people's skills professionally, giving responsibilities and developing leadership. Staff are appreciative of this encouragement to develop themselves professionally and the opportunities provided to take leadership responsibility.

b) Demonstrating interpersonal skills

The philosophy of headteacher and school is that each new initiative should be viewed as an opportunity for the school. He is able to win support and commitment through his interpersonal skills and the way he shows that he values the opinions and views of others. He:

- is open to different or contrary opinions or views

- attends weekly staff meetings with primary teachers and supports Quality Circles to generate ideas and take forward school concerns or issues

- acts quickly on requests and agreed actions

- gives staff autonomy and room to make decisions while at the same time being readily able to provide support when it is needed.

c) Developing personal credibility

By teaching in the classrooms and working regularly alongside teachers across the whole school, the headteacher has built up his credibility in the eyes of nursery, primary and secondary staff. Staff watch the headteacher teach and are consequently more relaxed about the headteacher seeing them teach. The headteacher leads by example.

- The headteacher and depute head secondary both take evening slots for pupils' supported study.

- A student profile has been built up for each S5 and S6 student with targets set for each student in each subject. Every student meets the headteacher every six weeks to review progress, providing a view of the school through the eyes of the students.

- The headteacher shares his expertise by delivering management and leadership courses for middle managers at weekends.

d) Developing teamwork

An advisory team, with promoted staff from the different sectors of the school, meets weekly to take forward policy development. This group gives the final approval to all school policies prior to implementation. There is an expectation that all staff will respond to all necessary consultation. This expectation is met by:

- evaluation of the work of the school being a key activity which informs the development planning process, surveys and questionnaires, based on the national performance indicators, are given to staff, parents and pupils

- buddy systems operating effectively, ground rules and responsibilities are agreed with the pupils and well laid out

- the school promoting an overall ethos of a family atmosphere from nursery through to secondary

- staff from nursery, primary and secondary working together in cross-sectoral groups to take forward initiatives

- the School Board playing a key role in looking at policy documents at the draft stage and putting forward ideas and views from the parental perspective

- the headteacher acknowledging that staff teamwork is essential in taking forward developments.

Impact and outcomes of leadership

The headteacher's leadership and vision have created a holistic approach to learning from 4 to 18 with strong links across all stages of the school. He has raised the value and self-esteem of all staff who are fully aware that he notices things and comments on good work. The HMI inspection highlighted:

- imaginative use of the limited accommodation in which staff had created a stimulating learning environment

- effective teaching and very good standards of attainment in national examinations

- high staff morale

- a very positive climate for professional review and staff development and a good match between individual staff development and school priorities

- target setting initiated for all pupils from S1 onwards.

How was this leadership developed?

The headteacher has made use of opportunities within the school to work alongside colleagues and to develop his own and others' leadership skills. He has also looked towards the education authority and national bodies as part of his professional development. For example by:

- attending various national courses for headteachers run by the Scottish Centre for Studies in School Administration (SCSSA)
- membership of education authority working parties, for example, on 5-14
- networking with other headteachers
- keeping up-to-date with developments in nursery, primary and secondary education
- working in each sector of the school to develop his own professional and teaching skills.

Next steps

A number of further steps have been identified as a further focus of leadership in the school:

- continuing the process of raising attainment
- challenging the next group of pupils and working out how to support each individual through the learning process
- trying to achieve the right balance between pressure and support, realism and high expectations
- drawing on national and education authority initiatives to act as a focus for team development at school level
- concentrating on monitoring the progress of each child from age 4 to age 18
- trying to ensure the pace of learning and expectations are right in S1 and S2.

Case Study 5: Leadership and quality assurance

Seafield Infant School   **West Lothian Council**

Background and context

Seafield Infant School has a roll of 20 pupils in a nursery class and 44 pupils at the P1-3 stages. At P4, pupils transfer to Murrayfield Primary School in the nearby town of Blackburn. The headteacher is Mrs Marjorie Morris who has been in post for 13 years. A recent HMI inspection of the school reported that, among a number of key strengths, quality assurance procedures for evaluating the work of the school were particularly strong.

Why was quality assurance an important focus for leadership?

- Experience in using SED Management Modules in the early 1990s convinced the headteacher of the importance of quality assurance procedures to improve overall practice.

- As a teaching head, she recognised that workable procedures to provide all staff with good quality information about pupils' progress and the general work of the school were a priority.

- She recognised the need to provide 'hard' evidence about the school's performance to herself, staff and education authority, rather than rely on professional instinct.

The nature of leadership in the school

The HMI Inspection reported that "the headteacher provided very good leadership and she had sound and up-to-date knowledge of curriculum issues and educational management". Leadership in the school is characterised by: **Being responsive; Being committed and purposeful; and Developing and sharing a vision.**

In relation to the focus on quality assurance, the characteristic that was particularly worthy of note was:

Being responsive

The headteacher has made a point of listening to the views of others to keep in touch with emerging issues and needs. She has tried to respond flexibly and creatively to further improve standards by:

- being open and up-front about management issues and her own approach to them

- consistently seeking the views of colleagues, taking note of them and keeping staff aware of what is under consideration

- providing what she refers to as a 'helicopter view' – an overview of provision that encourages teachers to set their practice in a wider-school context

- arranging formal and informal meetings to discuss how to gather evidence about the work of the school, consider findings and use them to meet pupils' needs

- consistently praising good work on the part of staff and pupils whenever it is observed so that all feel valued

- providing a clear lead in introducing colleagues, teaching and non-teaching, to the value of performance indicators

- inviting staff to use some performance indicators to evaluate aspects of their work that they knew were strong, so that they would appreciate the positive nature of this activity, before evaluating areas where there might be more weaknesses

- consulting staff fully on the creation of a three-year plan for evaluating all key areas

- sharing her regular monitoring with them on an on-going basis

- sharing the draft development plan with staff and involving them fully in taking forward the agreed priorities

- reporting progress in implementation of the plan once a year to the education authority, parents and staff.

Impact and outcomes of leadership

A commitment to ensuring quality in education became part of the staff's shared vision for the school and produced some very clear outcomes.

- The availability of up-to-date and detailed evidence about pupils' performance helped to ensure that programmes reflected the needs of individual pupils.

- The overall quality of learning and teaching is now good or very good as confirmed by the HMI report and the headteacher's on-gong monitoring. When pupils move to the next stage, a folder containing samples of their work provides added illustration of their prior attainment to complement the detailed assessment records.

- Pupils' attainment is consistently good or very good. Almost all P3 pupils achieve level A in reading, listening and mathematics. When comparing attainment to schools with similar characteristics, Seafield is within the top ten per cent.

Case Study 6: Leadership and teamwork

Auchenlodment Primary School   Renfrewshire Council

Background and context

Auchenlodment Primary School is located in Johnstone. It has a roll of 329 pupils in the P1-7 classes and 40 children in the nursery. The headteacher, Marion Burns, has been in post for seven years and has recently been appointed as an education adviser with Renfrewshire Council. A recent HMI inspection of the school reported that a key strength was the strong but sensitive leadership of the headteacher. It highlighted how she had encouraged a good sense of teamwork in developing all aspects of the work of the school.

Why was teamwork an important focus for leadership?

In her first year, the headteacher and staff carried out an audit and analysis of strengths, weaknesses, opportunities and threats (SWOT) related to the work of the school. The audit included staff discussion based on firm evidence and questionnaires issued to parents, staff and visitors.

One key point arising from the audit was that all staff were enthusiastic and wanted to be challenged and involved in school decision-making. There was also an agreed desire to raise the image and profile of the school in the local community. Together, the management team and all staff looked at the vision and aims for the school and linked these to the new development plan. In discussing the way ahead, it was agreed that the school's image and profile would only be improved if everyone worked together to achieve the vision. It was agreed that a key target in taking this priority forward was team building involving all teaching, support and ancillary staff to promote the school in the wider community.

The nature of leadership in the school

The headteacher has a clear view of her approach to creating an effective team and staff confirm this. It encompasses **Being responsive; Developing teamwork; Building alliances within and beyond the school; and Being committed and purposeful.** In relation to the focus on teamwork, the characteristic that was particularly worthy of note was:

Being committed and purposeful

The headteacher makes a point of listening carefully to children, staff, parents and the wider community and keeps closely in touch with emerging issues and needs. She responds flexibly and creatively, but consistently promotes standards and quality. This approach began in her first few weeks in the school and was promoted through the audit. It has continued through staff reviews, questionnaires to staff and visitors, consultation related to the development plan and overall school self-evaluation, especially of teaching and learning.

- The headteacher has a clear understanding of the context within which the school operates and systematically seeks out and develops productive partnerships in the immediate and wider community.
- All staff work together to build strong links with parents, the local community and support agencies.
- Productive links are being developed with local businesses which have supported the school through additional resources, improvements to the school environment and providing opportunities for staff development.
- Her energy is evident and she is proactive in identifying areas for improvement
- She has a strong, personal commitment to key priorities such as improving learning and teaching and pupil attainment.
- Her drive and commitment inspires and motivates others to give of their best.

Impact and outcomes of leadership

The positive effect of leadership in promoting the teamwork, involvement and development of staff was further confirmed when the school achieved an Investors in People (IiP) Award. The teamwork approach has benefited pupils and improved the school's image. Pupils are well motivated, work well together and are actively involved in their learning. Parents and staff generally take great pride in the school and all staff, including ancillary staff, promote the image of the school in the wider community.

Case Study 7: Leadership to raise attainment in English language and mathematics

Kingswells Primary School   **Aberdeen City Council**

Background and context

Kingswells Primary School serves the community of Kingswells, on the edge of Aberdeen. It was once a two-teacher village school but, following extensive new housing developments, the roll has grown rapidly to 320 primary pupils, with 80 children in the nursery. The headteacher, Isabel Bolton, took up post seven years ago and has led the school through major changes including moving the primary classes into a new, open-plan school. An HMI inspection reported that a key strength of the school was attainment levels which were consistently high across all areas of English language and mathematics.

Why was attainment in English language and mathematics an important focus for leadership?

Initial evaluations by the headteacher, using national test results and classroom observation, revealed some under-performance and levels of expectation that were not always appropriately set. Some other parts of the curriculum were relatively strong, for example, expressive arts. The headteacher felt that:

- it was essential for her, in her role as leader, to agree key priorities with staff at a time when the school was seeing rapid change in roll, new staff appointments and a move to a new building

- as many parents were new to both the area and the school, a declaration that a key focus would be on rigour in English language and mathematics would reassure them that the school was going to meet the needs of their children.

The nature of leadership in the school

The HMI inspection report stated that "the headteacher provided excellent leadership to the school". Some of the main leadership characteristics she displayed were: **Prioritising; Focusing on learning; Developing teamwork; and Personal credibility.**

In relation to the focus on raising attainment, the characteristic that was particularly worthy of note was:

Focusing on learning

The headteacher put pupils' learning at the centre of her leadership. The strategies she used to promote a climate of learning across the school included:

- setting challenging school targets through staff discussion which resulted in an agreed understanding of what Kingswells' pupils should achieve at each stage

- emphasising to staff that they were jointly accountable to each other for high standards in pupil achievement as much as to the headteacher

- encouraging teachers to share good practice and, if possible, to take on the role of curricular leaders

- giving a key role to assessment in raising achievement, including using senior teachers in a leading role to create a more formal assessment policy

- simplifying the recording of planning and assessment to enable teachers to record those pupils who exceeded or fell below agreed targets for their stage together with next steps

- rigorously monitoring pupils' attainment at all stages and using the analyses to help teachers to build individual pupil targets into their forward-plans

- introducing a national test forecast into forward-planning

- making staff development on learning and teaching a very high priority.

Impact and outcomes of leadership

The headteacher's clearly-focused approach to leadership has had many positive outcomes. The HMI report noted that the school was characterised by:

- a very high quality of learning and teaching

- very good attainment in English language and mathematics

- a very good ethos of achievement supported by all staff

- very well-structured programmes for all areas of the curriculum, ensuring a very good pace of progress.

Case Study 8: Leadership for continuous improvement

Laxdale Primary School   **Comhairle nan Eilean Siar**

Background and context

Laxdale Primary School serves the Laxdale area of Stornoway. It has a roll of 217 pupils including 43 in Gaelic-medium classes. The headteacher, Christina A MacDonald has been in post for 19 years. In a recent HMI inspection report, two key strengths of the school were found to be the very effective management and leadership of the headteacher and the notable commitment and teamwork of all staff. The school has recently achieved Investors in People (IiP) recognition.

Why was continuous improvement an important focus for leadership?

The school motto 'Working together for good' encapsulates the philosophy of the headteacher and the working practices of the whole-school community. The headteacher combines this philosophy with a drive for continuous improvement that is supported by all of the staff and recognised by parents and the community.

The nature of leadership in the school

Leadership in the school is characterised by: **Developing and sharing a vision; Focusing on learning; Developing teamwork; and Building alliances within and beyond the school.**

In relation to the focus on continuous improvement, one characteristic that was particularly worthy of note was:

Building alliances within and beyond the school

A focus of the headteacher's leadership has been to promote support for the school in the wider community. In the inspection, HMI reported a number of concerns with the accommodation and safety of the school building. The headteacher brought the community together to support the need for refurbishment of the school. She worked with the PTA and School Board along with the staff to lobby councillors and officials and to build up an enthusiasm and commitment to action. The whole community was represented at the education committee meeting where the decision on the refurbishment was considered. The School Board and PTA are strong and vibrant organisations and parents have been asked by other schools to go and talk to them about how to achieve such representation, commitment and enthusiasm.

A number of other initiatives have helped to build alliances.

- All staff serve on a working party and the importance of this involvement is stressed by the headteacher.

- Parents contribute to the whole-school team by taking full responsibility for organising support in the school library.

- Senior pupils have been offered responsibilities for a number of years in the school library, in looking after and helping younger pupils and in contributing to the school assembly. As part of the school's process of continuous improvement, the pupils were asked for their views on developing the responsibilities they were offered. Many of the pupils' ideas and suggestions were implemented.

Impact and outcomes of leadership

Well-planned innovation and on-going review are features of the school's operation. Doing and reviewing is a way of life in the school. All staff and pupils are involved in effective development planning to which there is effective input from the whole community. The school plan is used as a key working document by all staff. Many people associated with the school, including staff, parents and children, have opportunities to take responsibilities and make contributions. Each is encouraged and supported by the others in the school community. The school is a happy environment where high expectations are encouraged by frequent use of praise.

Case Study 9: Leadership and staff self-evaluation

Lochside Primary School   **Angus Council**

Background and context

Val Beattie is depute headteacher in Lochside Primary School in Montrose and has been in post three years. The school has a roll of 400 pupils, 18 of whom have special educational needs. Fourteen of those with special educational needs have Records of Needs. A further 80 pupils attend two half-day nursery classes. Prior to her appointment as depute headteacher, she was a senior teacher in the school, responsible for setting up and managing the nursery unit.

The context for this case study is the development of self-evaluation strategies in the school. The depute headteacher played a leading role in this development, working closely with the assistant headteacher, and using the effective leadership of the headteacher as a role model. A recent HMI inspection of the school reported that:

"Self-evaluation strategies in the school were well established. The depute headteacher and assistant headteacher monitored the structure and delivery of work, collaborating with teachers at the planning stage and regularly working with them in the classroom. Teachers had made a good start to using performance indicators to evaluate aspects of learning and teaching in their classes. They regularly discussed their work with colleagues and with promoted staff".

Why was staff self-evaluation an important focus for leadership?

The main reasons for a focus on self-evaluation were to:

- establish a quality culture at all levels within the school
- ensure that staff were fully involved in school development planning.

The nature of leadership in the school

The depute headteacher displayed the following leadership characteristics: **Prioritising; Focusing on learning; and Being responsive.**

In relation to the focus on staff self-evaluation, one characteristic that was particularly worthy of note was:

Prioritising

Working closely with senior colleagues, and consulting with staff, the depute headteacher exercised good leadership by:

- focusing teacher self-evaluation initially on the key areas of learning and teaching and overall attainment, using appropriate performance indicators

- using the existing six-weekly, forward-planning cycle as the main vehicle for self-evaluation

- using the Level 4 illustrations in selected performance indicators to develop a checklist of key features of good classroom practice

- encouraging teachers at these six-weekly intervals to select some key features in the checklist, offer an evaluation of practice in their own classroom and suggest possible developments for the teacher or the school as a whole

- following up such discussion by working in classes to observe practice

- refining the process, after an initial pilot phase, by identifying the aspects to be evaluated each six-weekly cycle across the school

- summarising the main findings of the self-evaluation

- raising relevant issues at senior management meetings

- feeding the main findings into the school development planning group to ensure that the main priorities in the school plan took full account of the staff's overall self-evaluation.

Impact and outcomes of leadership

Well-structured school development plans were founded clearly on the outcomes of the school's self-evaluation process and made a significant contribution to school improvement. As a result, a good quality Standards and Quality report has been produced, providing an overall evaluation of all seven key areas. The staff experience of self-evaluation using performance indicators has increased staff confidence in relation to quality assurance.

Case Study 10: Leadership focused on improving subject examination performance

Balfron High School   **Stirling Council**

Background and context

Balfron High School has a roll of 849 and serves a large rural catchment area in West Stirlingshire. The principal teacher of biology is Jim Shields who has held the post for seven years. An HMI inspection of biology and S1/2 science identified one of the key strengths as "very high standards of attainment in biology courses at all levels".

Why was improved examination performance an important focus for leadership?

The principal teacher wanted to:

- increase the numbers opting for the subject at S3-S6
- raise the subject's status amongst pupils, parents and staff
- ensure that every pupil's needs were met with an appropriate level of challenge.

The nature of leadership in the department

HMI reported that the principal teacher was "a highly effective leader". In his general work, many of the ten leadership characteristics were in evidence. In this context, the main leadership characteristics were: **Being committed and purposeful; Prioritising; Focusing on learning; and Developing personal credibility.** In relation to the focus on improving subject examination performance, one characteristic which was particularly worthy of note was:

Developing personal credibility

The principal teacher has demonstrated effective professional expertise in his day-to-day work by:

- using six years of post-graduate research and 15 years of teaching experience to develop his extensive knowledge of the subject
- committing time and energy to becoming highly involved in national developments such as Higher Still; he has been involved in the delivery of in-service courses at local and national level and has worked with the Scottish Qualifications Authority in the writing of unit and course assessment items
- meeting his key departmental responsibilities effectively, particularly in evaluating progress, monitoring attainment, planning for improvement, budgeting efficiently and meeting deadlines.

He is a reliable source of information and advice to colleagues on educational practice. He ensures that he demonstrates hands-on leadership and the ability to translate aims into reality by:

- using his up-to-date knowledge of developments such as Higher Still to offer practical advice to teachers

- taking every opportunity, informally and at planned meetings, to initiate discussion on teaching and assessment approaches

- making himself approachable and indicating a willingness to share information about new research and developments in the subject

- trialling new approaches such as practical activities in Higher Still courses

- using resources in a targeted way to meet key priorities.

He tries to develop good practice by personal example through:

- showing an enjoyment in teaching

- continually seeking improvements in his course planning and teaching and learning approaches

- being fully involved with pupils' learning throughout every lesson

- showing that the classroom is his first and main priority

- making clear he has high but realistic expectations of every pupil.

Impact and outcomes of leadership

The biology department is very well regarded in the school. Pupils' attainment is high. The HMI report on attainment in biology showed that, over the last five years, the proportion of pupils in Standard Grade gaining a Credit award was more than double the national average. The proportion of S5 pupils gaining A awards at Higher Grade was more than three times the national average. The uptake of NC modules was high with most pupils successfully completing all learning outcomes, and in CSYS courses almost all pupils obtained A-C passes.

Case Study 11: Leadership to promote teamwork

Banff Academy   **Aberdeenshire Council**

Background and context

Banff Academy is a six-year secondary school in Aberdeenshire. The school has a roll of 1,100 pupils and 80 teachers. The headteacher, George Sinclair, has been in post for six and a half years. He is a former pupil of the school and also began his teaching career there. A recent HMI inspection report on the school referred to "very good teamwork within the senior management team". It also identified as a major strength "a strong, positive consensus amongst staff for the programme of change the school was undergoing".

Why was teamwork an important focus for leadership?

Experience in previous posts had convinced the headteacher of the positive gains that a school would accrue if good teamwork were a strong feature. When appointed to Banff Academy, he was strongly of the view that this should be a key feature of management. This clear appreciation of the fact that no one person has all the answers prompted him to lay down strong foundations for teamwork at all levels in the school.

The nature of leadership in the school

The HMI inspection report noted that a key strength of the school was the very good and effective leadership provided by the headteacher. The headteacher displayed the following leadership characteristics: **Delegating and sharing leadership; Developing teamwork; and Demonstrating interpersonal skills.**

In relation to the focus, one characteristic that was particularly worthy of note was:

Developing teamwork

Underlying values and collaborative ways of working are seen as important in promoting the development of teamwork in the school.

Within the senior management team:

- the overall school values, beliefs and school direction are clear and shared
- the tone is informal and relaxed
- mutual respect and good humour are evident
- discussion may be initiated by any member of the team and is not dominated by the headteacher
- disagreements are encouraged with the positive and negative aspects teased out

- discussion usually continues until a clear strategy emerges and only when differences cannot be reconciled does the headteacher decide

- once agreements are reached, responsibilities are allocated and targets set.

In setting up staff working groups to agree and revise policy, the headteacher:

- takes care to choose an issue arising from the staff's evaluation of provision and writes a clear remit for the group

- selects membership of working groups to include a balanced mix of subject backgrounds, experience, age, position and views

- chooses the chairperson with considerable care, with an eye on the person's credibility and ability to build a team

- involves himself, or an SMT colleague, as a member and a support for the group

- allows the group to choose how to work.

Although no group has ever come up with proposals that could have been precisely predicted from the outset, the headteacher has always been able to accept the recommendations and proposals of school working groups. This is seen as a strength of the system and endorsement of the team approach.

Impact and outcomes of leadership

The concern to promote teamwork, delegate and share leadership widely are now established as key features in the school. Important aspects of the very effective leadership of the senior management team include:

- strong corporate responsibility
- effective mutual support
- highly-visible leadership by the whole team around the school
- effective links with departments to promote quality in learning and teaching
- involvement of staff at all levels in effective teamwork.

Case Study 12: Leadership to develop co-operation among staff

Bannerman High School   **Glasgow City Council**

Background and context

Bannerman High School serves the Baillieston area in the east of Glasgow. It has a roll of 1,450 and a teaching complement of 99 FTE. The headteacher, Iain Duncan, has been in post for ten years. A recent HMI inspection noted that the headteacher's thoughtful, analytical approach, knowledge of staff and effective delegation were particular strengths. The depute headteacher and assistant headteachers carried out their challenging duties very well. Together with the headteacher, they formed a very strong, committed senior management team.

Why was co-operation among staff an important focus for leadership?

The headteacher reflected on his career in teaching and management, and considered that the most effective schools he had experienced were those in which teamwork, co-operation and sharing were strong features. He shared his aims and vision with the staff and worked with them to set out procedures to inform the working of the school. This encompassed communication and consultation mechanisms that would involve all staff. Policy development and new initiatives would be taken forward through groups of staff taking responsibility for the work, but always linking back to the rest of the staff for feedback and discussion at critical stages.

The nature of leadership in the school

The HMI report noted that the headteacher provided very good leadership. In particular, the following leadership characteristics are evident: **Being responsive; Demonstrating interpersonal skills; Developing teamwork; and Developing personal credibility.**

In relation to the focus on developing staff collaboration, one characteristic that was particularly worthy of note was:

Demonstrating interpersonal skills

The headteacher's approach demonstrates the importance of interpersonal skills including:

- significant self-reflection on his own strengths and areas for development
- 'management by walking about' involving frequently being around the school to visit classes and to engage staff in discussions about the developing school agenda

- recognising how hard staff are working and providing recognition of their achievements
- demonstrating good negotiating skills through valuing other people's opinions and listening to opposing views.

The headteacher and management team are skilled at empowering teams and individuals to take developments forward whilst at the same time keeping in touch with the progress being made and the support needed.

Impact and outcomes of leadership

The HMI report highlighted that effective leadership had resulted in a number of key strengths in the school, including:

- the well thought-out approach to policy-making
- opportunities for all staff to be involved through responding to consultation and serving on committees
- committed and hard-working staff
- the many examples of very good teaching
- the strengths of senior and departmental management.

Case Study 13: Leadership to promote an ethos of achievement

Larbert High School   **Falkirk Council**

Background and context

Larbert High School serves the communities of Larbert, Stenhousemuir, Carron, Carronshore, Airth, Skinflats and the surrounding area. The school roll is 1,472 pupils. The headteacher, Rosemary Holmes, took up post in 1993. The school operates on a split site. This has posed considerable problems, though building work is currently under way to bring the school together on one site. The context for this case study is the strong ethos of achievement in the school. Pupils and staff have a clear sense of purpose and high expectations of behaviour and achievement. A recent HMI inspection reported that:

"The pupils and staff identified very strongly with the school and took pride in it. Many staff expected high standards of work and pupils responded very well. The school was working hard to promote an ethos of achievement and its efforts were meeting with success".

Why was an ethos of achievement an important focus for leadership?

The headteacher saw potential for development both in terms of staff's ability to achieve a positive ethos and in their willingness to change. She saw that an ethos of achievement, characterised by high expectations, was the best way to recognise pupils' good behaviour, to improve their self-esteem and to raise their overall attainment and achievement.

The nature of leadership in the school

HMI found that "the headteacher was highly committed and provided very good leadership for the school". The main characteristics of her leadership in this context include: **Developing and sharing a vision; Developing teamwork; and Developing personal credibility.**

In relation to the focus on promoting an ethos of achievement, one characteristic that was particularly worthy of note was:

Developing and sharing a vision

The headteacher has developed a vision for the school with a clear sense of purpose, a shared sense of direction and an ethos of achievement by:

- consulting widely with staff, pupils and parents to agree appropriate school aims

- displaying these aims prominently, including various pupil versions in a variety of layouts, in the main school entrances, in all classrooms and on noticeboards, in order to get across what is seen as really important

- producing a quality school development plan as a main vehicle for introducing changes in a planned way

- working with staff to develop and put into place a policy to promote pupils' positive behaviour and adding, over the years, various refinements and improvements. This scheme has many impressive features including:

  - a standard of good behaviour shared with the pupils
  - pupils made fully aware that they have an important part to play in the school's success
  - pupil successes celebrated in notices at the school entrance, weekly house assemblies and an annual awards ceremony
  - weekly recognition of the best class in attendance
  - classroom conduct codes in all classrooms, good conduct vouchers and stickers and congratulatory letters sent home
  - displays of the involvement of the wider community to demonstrate the support and goodwill the school enjoys.

- regularly sharing the vision of a high-achieving school with high expectations with each pupil through:

  - the use of a monitoring report
  - a follow-up discussion with the pupil or the parents
  - an individual interview that celebrates success, reviews progress and sets targets
  - a supported study scheme with transport provided for pupils living outwith the town
  - a mentoring scheme for vulnerable pupils, using staff volunteers trained for the role.

Impact and outcomes of leadership

The headteacher's approach in promoting an ethos of achievement has had many positive outcomes.

- The Improving School Effectiveness Project (ISEP) statistics showed that in Larbert High School, staff responses to the statement that "pupil success is regularly celebrated in the school" were 99 per cent compared to the average response in other project schools of 65 per cent. Also, 78 per cent of the staff felt that "the SMT communicated a clear vision", a figure 23 per cent higher than the average response.

- HMI reported that "relationships between staff and pupils were generally very good and staff morale was high. Most classes were very orderly and purposeful".

- Attainment in 5 plus Credit awards at Standard Grade and 3 plus A - C awards at Higher Grade has shown a rising trend over the past few years.

- The absence rate has been reduced over the past five years.

- The number of exclusions has declined and the school has successfully extended its range of strategies to manage challenging behaviour.

Case Study 14: Leadership to develop primary - secondary liaison

Webster's High School   **Angus Council**

Background and context

Webster's High School is the secondary school serving the town of Kirriemuir and the surrounding rural area. The roll is 754. The principal teacher of Support for Learning is Jeanette Smeaton, who has held the post for 13 years. A recent HMI report on the school noted that:

"The principal teacher of Support for Learning provided leadership of high quality. She was energetic and committed, and had a clear view of how the effectiveness of the school's Support for Learning provision should be developed. She was particularly successful in motivating staff and encouraging good teamwork".

The context for this case study is a new project the school identified to raise standards. Funding was provided by the education authority for an additional Support for Learning teacher. This extra staffing allowance enabled the Support for Learning department to timetable regular contact throughout the school year with all ten associated primary schools. The aims of this project were to strengthen links and improve the quality of information available to secondary teachers about the new S1 intake. The headteacher suggested this idea and delegated the leadership of the project to the principal teacher.

Why was primary-secondary liaison an important focus for leadership?

The principal teacher welcomed the opportunity to lead the project. It was very much in accord with her own vision whereby new S1 pupils, who had benefited from extra support in the primary school, would be sufficiently well known to secondary staff to ensure a smooth and positive transition. She aimed for a position where the support provided to pupils in their new setting would be seamless and closely targeted on their known needs.

The nature of leadership in the school

The principal teacher, working closely with senior management, was considered by all involved to have brought very effective leadership to this project. The key leadership characteristics displayed were: **Building alliances within and beyond the school; and Delegating and sharing leadership.**

In relation to the focus on primary-secondary liaison, one characteristic that was particularly worthy of note was:

Delegating and sharing leadership

The headteacher had delegated to the principal teacher the leadership of this new initiative. In turn, she shared leadership with others through effective delegation. In particular, she:

- took opportunities to work collaboratively to build up a more detailed profile on every pupil and improve curricular continuity
- gained approval from all involved - headteachers and class teachers in the primaries and senior management and principal teachers in the secondary school
- arranged other secondary colleagues in five subject areas to work with primary teachers and classes on joint curricular projects
- arranged for all six Support for Learning colleagues to be linked with one or more primary schools for part of each week
- built up an accurate and detailed profile of each pupil through a process involving mainly team teaching.

Impact and outcomes of leadership

The main outcomes for the primary schools included:

- improved transfer procedures
- improved links with, and curricular support from, secondary subject departments
- reassurance that the pupil profiles that the primaries built up were being well used by all secondary teachers
- more effective support for learning provision.

The main outcomes for the secondary school included:

- a much improved profile of information on every S1 pupil to be shared with every secondary teacher
- Support for Learning staff better prepared than before to deliver effective support as soon as new S1 pupils arrived
- improved curricular co-ordination in modern languages, science, mathematics, English and social subjects.

Training in leadership and management

The ten key leadership characteristics can be developed through formal training which takes different forms. Two examples are outlined below.

The Scottish Qualification for Headship

The Scottish Qualification for Headship (SQH) is a new qualification which has been introduced to ensure that people who wish to become headteachers can obtain the development opportunities they need prior to appointment. The qualification is designed to develop and improve participants' practice as school leaders and managers. It involves not only attending courses and workshops, but also a large element of work-based learning. With this blend of learning, the SQH programme is delivered on the basis of a partnership between local authorities and licensed providers. The purpose of the SQH programme is to enable candidates to develop the competencies they need in order to achieve the Standard for Headship in Scotland. The Standard specifies the key purposes of headship and the professional values, management functions and professional abilities which describe competence in headship.

The programme started in 1998 as a pilot and will become fully operational in session 2000-2001. It is open to those who have five years or more teaching experience. Candidates are selected for the programme by their employers on the basis that they have already shown the potential to develop the competencies required for effective school leadership and management.

Meeting the criteria for the Standard involves the candidate going through a process which has three main stages:

- assessment against the Standard
- the implementation of school projects which will allow the candidate to develop the professional competencies required to carry out the key competencies of school leadership and management successfully
- demonstration to the key purpose of headship.

Overall, the programme would normally be expected to take two to three years to complete. However, candidates may opt for an accelerated route and complete the programme within one year.

Case studies 15 and 16 are of two candidates, one from the primary sector and one from the secondary, who opted for the accelerated route during the pilot phase and were successful in gaining the qualification.

Courses provided by education authorities

A number of education authorities provide courses on leadership and management. These can be of particular value in developing leadership at all levels within schools. Case studies 9 and 14 are of delegates who attended 'Keys to management' courses delivered by Angus Council. They offer an account of how this formal training assisted their leadership development when back in school.

Training in leadership (SQH)

Case Study 15: Depute headteacher   Edinburgh City Council

Background and context

Tynecastle High School serves a catchment area in the south west of Edinburgh. The depute headteacher is Dr John Campbell who took up post after having had three and a half years senior management experience as an assistant headteacher in a previous school.

Why did he wish to gain this qualification?

- He wanted to be a headteacher and wished to prepare professionally for that role.
- He engaged regularly in other staff development and had also undertaken other professional studies in education.
- He wanted to explore his own practice.
- He felt that the training would help him to follow up the recommendations arising from his review.
- He wanted to build on what he felt was substantial experience in managing core operations in schools.

Developing leadership

Leadership skills have been developed in a number of ways during his career. In his view, the SQH programme made a particularly significant contribution to his professional development by helping him to:

- have opportunities for personal reflection
- become more aware of the important leadership role of the headteacher and recognise more clearly the demanding position a headteacher occupied
- recognise the importance of developing a vision and guard against being overly pragmatic
- learn how to communicate his vision to others
- know what his basic educational values were.

Other influences on his leadership development have included:

- five years as a youth and community worker in an inner-city area before training as a teacher which shaped his leadership style and helped him realise that the needs of young people must always be put at the forefront

- ten years of part-time study for further educational qualifications
- advice of critical friends, including his present headteacher and other senior staff who meet together as a neighbourhood group.

Next steps

A number of further steps will assist in the development of leadership:

- acting as headteacher during the school session 1999/2000, including leading the school through an HMI inspection
- developing the new senior management team which included two acting appointments
- putting a clear focus on learning by re-emphasising the importance of learning and teaching as the core activities of the school
- sharing leadership with principal teachers by devolving more responsibility to them for managing discussion forums set up to review school issues and policies
- giving increased recognition to the important contribution non-teaching staff make to effective team working in the school
- access to the City of Edinburgh Council's management development opportunities.

Training in leadership (SQH)

Case Study 16: Headteacher   **Glasgow City Council**

Background and context

Ann Robertson is headteacher of Craigton Primary School, Glasgow. She was appointed to this post in October 1999. She undertook the Scottish Qualification for Headship during the school session 1998/99 when she was depute headteacher in Elder Park Primary School, Glasgow. She chose the accelerated route to study for the qualification.

Why did she wish to gain this qualification?

- She wanted to be a headteacher and wished to prepare for that responsibility by engaging in professional training.

- She had six years experience as a depute headteacher and felt she was now confident in that role and the responsibilities associated with it.

- In acting as headteacher on several occasions, she had become very aware of the need for improved knowledge about some important areas of school management.

- The participation of the school in the Investors in People (IiP) scheme, resulting in the IiP award, gave her a role as staff development co-ordinator and opportunities to reflect on her management and leadership.

- As the staff development co-ordinator, she was very convinced of the value to colleagues and herself of good quality staff development.

Why the accelerated route?

She had the benefits of:

- extensive management experience as a depute headteacher
- a good model of leadership provided by her headteacher at the time.

Although she was prepared for a demanding workload, she found the accelerated route more intense and demanding than she anticipated, and reported that "it took over my life for a year".

Developing leadership

Her leadership has been shaped in a variety of ways.

In her view, the SQH programme made a particularly significant contribution to her leadership development by:

- demonstrating the importance of looking beyond the day-to-day running of the school and having a long-term vision
- reinforcing the necessity for this vision to be shared and suggesting ways in which the vision could become a reality using careful strategic and short-term planning
- emphasising the importance of developing effective teamwork
- giving opportunities to evaluate one's own practice, identifying strengths and areas requiring further development.

Other influences on her leadership included:

- the very good leadership model of her former headteacher, especially with regard to developing participative management and the sharing of a vision for the school
- the scope given to her through effective delegation to use her own initiative and judgement
- three reviews as a depute headteacher which helped her to recognise some successes in that role and identified some important development needs
- advice and support sought from, and readily given by, education authority advisers
- opportunities to deliver a course for others in managing staff development which gave further opportunities for reflection on her practice as a co-ordinator and leader
- management training courses offered by the education authority and, in particular, the unit on "Principles on Management".

Next steps

As a newly-appointed headteacher, she has now set out to:

- have a clear sense of purpose and a strong commitment to school priorities
- develop productive relationships with staff, parents, outside agencies and the wider community
- encourage others to become involved in the decision-making processes through participative management structures
- promote a climate of evaluation which allows good practice to be shared and maintains the focused aim of improving pupil learning
- prioritise effectively, and agree with staff, a sustainable pace for making changes through effective development planning
- use continuous professional development to allow her to develop her own skills, be familiar with current educational issues and be a knowledgeable role model for staff.

Designed and produced on behalf of the Scottish Executive by Tactica Solutions 6/00 B11146